Ms. Karen Johnson
24 Laurie Ln
Westminster, MA 01473

PARTING VISIONS

PARTING VISIONS

USES AND MEANINGS OF PRE-DEATH, PSYCHIC, AND SPIRITUAL EXPERIENCES

Melvin Morse, M.D.,
with Paul Perry

WITH AN INTRODUCTION BY BETTY J. EADIE

VILLARD BOOKS ▪ NEW YORK ▪ 1994

Library of Congress Cataloging-in-Publication Data
Morse, Melvin.
Parting visions: uses and meanings of pre-death, psychic, and spiritual experiences/by
Melvin Morse with Paul Perry; introduction by Betty J. Eadie.
p.   cm.
ISBN 0-679-42754-6
1. Near-death experiences.   I. Perry, Paul.   II. Title.
BF1045.N4M675   1994   33.9′ 01′ 3—dc20   94-21272

For Diane Reverand,
who has made our work possible

PROLOGUE

The term *death-related visions* is a general label for the broad category of spiritual experiences that take place in the arena of death. They are paranormal experiences that happen to normal people. Death-related visions include such events as near-death experiences, after-death visitations, and healing visions. Also included are precognitive experiences, dreams, visions, and other premonitions of death that come true. I sometimes refer to these death-related visions as spiritual experiences. I don't use this term in a religious sense, but rather as a means of describing the non-ordinary reality of visionary encounters. These visions have an awe-inspiring effect on our spirits. I have never met a person, no matter how cynical, who is not in some way intrigued by the meaning of these parting visions.

Few death-related visions sum up their total impact better than what happened to Lizabeth Sumner.

Lizabeth is a veteran of hospice work. This down-to-earth nurse and mother works in the San Diego Hospice in California. There she has helped more than one hundred people take their final journey into death.

Her long-term exposure to death and dying makes Lizabeth's experience even more extraordinary than most. The death-related vision of a mother who has lost a child can easily be discounted as a "grief-induced hallucination," but when a veteran health care worker has such a vision, it is not so easy for the skeptical to write off the experience as wish fulfillment. In this case the fact that another person many miles away shared the experience makes it even harder to dismiss.

This supernatural story begins in the most natural of ways. Around Valentine's Day Lizabeth was busy helping a little boy die. He had a form of heart disease, and the doctors had done everything they could to prolong his life. Now that the end was near, this boy—we will call him Jimmy—had decided to die at home.

His parents supported his decision to die at home. They had seen him struggle for a long time, and now they knew it was his time to die. They surrounded him with love and tried to make his last days as comfortable as possible.

Lizabeth came to help. As a hospice nurse she frequently found herself visiting people's homes, where she administered medicine to the dying and gave the family some rest from the strain of caring for the terminally ill.

Lizabeth took a special liking to Jimmy and his family. They were tight-knit and caring, and Jimmy showed much of the confidence and intelligence of a child who was raised by supportive parents.

Jimmy and his family gave everything they had to each other in his last days. They celebrated his ninth birthday on Valentine's Day, a few months early, because they knew he wouldn't make it to the actual date. His only birthday wish was to go to dinner in a limousine. Although they were fairly poor, Jimmy's parents did the best they could, renting a black Lincoln because they couldn't afford an actual limo. The whole family rode around town as Jimmy basked in the front seat of the car.

He liked the car and said that he wished he could buy one for his family. When they stopped for dinner, it was at a convenience market, where they ate hot dogs and drank Slurpees. For a while it was as though he had forgotten that this was his last birthday party.

Later he wrote Valentine notes to all of his friends and put them in envelopes. He also enclosed tiny gold crosses he had purchased and asked that they be used to remember him by.

The actual death a few weeks later was not a surprise. His mother said that he got up early that morning to make sandwiches for his brothers' school lunches. "I want to make sure their sandwiches are special today," he told his mother. "They are going to need all the energy they can get."

Jimmy weakened as the day progressed. He went into the living room to lie down. He asked that his favorite music be put on his tape player as he lay there. The fight was fading out of his eyes by now. Lizabeth could see that it was Jimmy's time to let go and die. She monitored his vital signs and gave him what aid and comfort she could.

By sundown Jimmy was actively dying. His heartbeat was fluctuating, and there were periods where he seemed to slip into a coma.

Lizabeth marveled at how much dying resembled the birthing process. Music was playing, and the parents embraced Jimmy. "Come on," they said. "Come on, now, it's all right, Jimmy. It's okay to let go." For a moment Jimmy would seem to leave his body. Then he would pull back in, and the spark of life would show again on his face. Finally he became weaker and weaker as his parents held him closer. Then he sighed and left his body for good, surrounded by his brothers, parents, pediatrician, and Lizabeth.

Lizabeth's job was almost over now.

She helped the family make some of the necessary phone calls and waited for the mortuary van to arrive. When she noticed that one of Jimmy's brothers was standing alone in the front yard, she took a basketball outside and shot hoops with him to help make him feel better. About half an hour later she left for home.

That was when it happened.

As she drove down the freeway, the windshield was suddenly filled with a vision so vivid that she had to pull off to the side of the road.

In this vision she saw Jimmy, happy and animated, holding a man's hand. She couldn't see whose hand he was holding, but Jimmy was happy. He looked adoringly toward the man's face and had a look of great peace. The vision was as real as a moving picture and continued for as long as one minute. No words were spoken by the boy, but his eyes said it all as far as Lizabeth was concerned. "The life was back in his bright blue eyes and he was very comfortable," said Lizabeth. "I could hear him say, 'I'm alright now,' without him moving his lips."

Lizabeth told only her husband about the vision. She thought of keeping it that way, but what she had seen was so vivid that she felt she had to tell someone else. She thought she should at least tell Jimmy's family. Certainly they would find comfort in what she had seen.

After the funeral Lizabeth pulled Jimmy's mother aside. They were standing outside the cemetery next to a tree when Lizabeth told the mother what she had seen. The woman immediately burst into tears.

"That's exactly what my husband saw," she said. "Right after Jimmy died, my husband saw the same thing."

———

This story captures the power of death-related visions. They are paranormal events that possess an enormous potential for healing.

Everyone associated with Jimmy felt healed by this vision, from the family to all of the health care workers who heard the story. After such a long and drawn-out death process, this story brought everyone comfort.

That this experience could happen to a veteran health care worker who had seen many people die as well as to loving family members exposed for the first time to death was an added confirmation that something unexplainable had indeed happened. Even medical doctors who were told this story withheld their skepticism, an unusual reaction. Even though millions of people have had death-related visions, it is rare to find a medical doctor who takes such visions seriously. A patient who reports such a vision will most likely be told that it is a hallucination or some kind of wish fulfillment, in which a person thinks he sees a departed loved one simply because he wants to. Most doctors do not regard these visions to be what they are — medicine for the soul, or maybe *from* the soul.

Whatever their origin, death-related visions are powerful medicine, capable of affecting body and mind alike. Because of their healing powers alone they deserve rigorous study.

Scientific research can be difficult and arduous. Once it becomes connected with spiritual matters, the reaction against it by the scientific and medical community can be astounding. Science changes slowly. For instance, only recently has the medical community admitted that something as simple as positive thinking could actually speed the healing process. It took years of scientific research to convince them of that.

Now that the powers of the mind to speed healing have been proven, medical doctors of all ages have spread the word to their patients. Millions of people now pursue new medical modalities such as biofeedback and even prayer as part of their recovery from illness. They have done so because research has made a verifiable fact of this longtime belief. In short, medical research has made something tangible out of the intangible.

The same has been true of near-death experiences. For years these fascinating experiences were nothing more than myth. They received attention as fodder for talk shows, but they were not taken seriously by the medical community until the late 1970s, when Dr. Raymond Moody published an informal study that showed the elements common to all near-death experiences.

Even then most doctors ridiculed them. When I conducted my studies into the near-death experiences of children, for instance, my fellow doctors would whistle the theme to *The Twilight Zone* as they walked passed me in the halls of the hospital.

I took this musical accompaniment to my studies in cautious good humor. It was clear that their jokes had an edge to them. Finally one of my colleagues hit the issue head-on: "Mel," he said. "If you are going to study something that even hints at life after death, you had better make sure your science is pretty damn good."

I took his advice. Now my work has been published in some of the world's most prestigious medical journals, where it was subjected to the scrutiny of peer review before publication. The same has happened to the near-death research of many other scientists. Our findings have now become institutionalized and are already appearing in textbooks and in medical school lectures. Patients who have near-death experiences no longer have to worry about being branded mentally ill or "weird." Instead medical schools now teach that the near-death experience is a natural and normal part of life, and doctors everywhere are removing their intellectual blinders.

This book looks at the broader range of death-related visions. For more than a decade I have been hearing these cases from patients, readers, nurses, and even my fellow medical doctors. Most of them begin their stories by saying, "You might think I am crazy, but . . . ," and then go on to tell a story that is anything but lunacy. These people have been healed by their visions, some even renewed, but still they doubt their own experience because of social and cultural conditioning.

At first I doubted the validity of death-related visions too. Like most doctors, I didn't think that such experiences happened to normal people. Then I began to listen with an open mind and realized that these people were not crazy. As I listened, I began to hear more stories, and the more I heard, the more I analyzed. It became clear to me that these stories had merit. I also realized that there is clearly a gap in understanding when it comes to visions. As a result we are missing an opportunity to use the human spirit as an effective tool for healing.

This book is a step toward bridging that gap. As a pediatrician with a busy clinical practice, I am interested in anything that can make life better for my patients. As a researcher in the field of near-death studies, I am intrigued at the possibility of our having the capacity to understand things in ways that we don't yet comprehend. I brought the two disciplines of clinical practice and my research interests together to arrive at some remarkable conclusions about these visions.

I have also collected a number of visions in this book and

analyzed their content from my point of view. You might arrive at different conclusions from mine. I expect that. After all, I do not pretend that this book has all the answers, but at least it begins to address the questions.

—Melvin Morse, M.D.

CONTENTS

CONTENTS

INTRODUCTION

BY BETTY J. EADIE, AUTHOR OF *EMBRACED BY THE LIGHT*

I have told very few people the spiritual experiences I am about to relate here. I want to share them with you now because you will read about many just like them in this courageous and insightful book.

The first one has to do with my daughter, Cynthia, who died at the age of three months of sudden infant death syndrome (SIDS).

Usually I would hold her just until she fell asleep and then put her to bed. I had several children already, and as any parent in that position knows, I needed all the spare time I could get. When I got her to sleep, I finally had some time to myself to rest.

This particular night was different. When Cynthia fell asleep, I held her in my arms for several hours. Even though I had other things to do, I felt deeply compelled on this particular night just to hold her in my arms and rock her.

She died later that night.

Parents have a special bond with their children. I have heard many parents tell of knowing that their children were in trouble, even when they were hundreds of miles away from one another. This is a psychic bond that most parents admit to without hesitation.

In this book you will find scientific proof of this bond. As one of the investigators in a study of parents who lost children to SIDS, Melvin Morse has helped to show that premonitions of a child's death are common occurrences that happen to "normal" people. He has helped to prove scientifically that this psychic bond between parent and child is a real one, not one of make-believe.

I believe that premonitions are God's way of telling us about difficult events before they happen so that they will not come as such a surprise to us. God does not give us more than we can handle, and one of his ways of doing that is by gracing us with visions that foreshadow events.

He did that with me just a few days before my father died. The visions I had took place in a dream. I was puzzled by its symbolic content when it happened, but after my father died, there was no mistaking what it meant.

The dream began with the entire family's gathering at a local park for my father's surprise birthday party. I asked them to wait outside the fence while I went in to see how the preparations were going.

I walked through the gate and down to a house where this party was to be held. On a table inside I saw a beautiful cake that was two tiers high. It was tall and frosted beautifully like a wedding cake. On top was a single candle and next to it a beautiful little angel with wings.

The cake was breathtaking. As I stood admiring it, my husband said, "That's nothing, wait until you see this."

He lit the candle and stood back. The angel fluttered its wings and turned toward the candle. Then, with a gentle puff of air, it blew out the candle.

I was delighted. "Light it again," I said.

My husband lit the candle, and the angel fluttered to life again, extinguishing the flame with a sweet puff.

I wanted to see more. "Do it again," I insisted. Once again my husband obliged. He lit the candle, and the angel did her job, offering a puff that turned the flame to smoke for the third time.

I was distracted from the cake by the arrival of several men with clipboards. They approached me and asked for a family history.

I didn't know who they were and asked why they were there. "This is a birthday party," one of them said. "But also a sort of family reunion," said another. "We need some information about the family background."

I spoke freely to them.

Finally it was time for the party, and the guests began to arrive. My children began to show up one by one, until the only one missing was one of my daughters, Donna.

"Why isn't she here?" I said. "She had better get here soon, or the party is going to be over."

As the time of the party drew near, she finally called. Something had happened, she said, and she would be about an hour late. I was irritated. "You had better get here soon, or the party is going to be over," I said.

That is where the dream ended.

A few days later the meaning of this dream became painfully obvious to me.

I went to a restaurant for breakfast with my father. We

placed our order and were served our coffee. My father asked me to pass him the sugar. I reached for the container at the end of the table. When I turned back around, his chin had slumped to his chest.

I jumped up from my chair and ran around to hold him. As I did, three puffs of air came out of his mouth that were identical to the sounds made by the angel that blew out the candle in my dream.

Emergency services were called. Medics arrived and put my father on a stretcher for the trip to the hospital. As I watched helplessly, one of the medics approached me with a clipboard and asked questions about my father's health history.

At the hospital he was placed on a ventilator, but it soon became painfully clear that he was brain-dead. There was nothing the doctors could do. They suggested that we remove him from life support and let him die.

I wanted the entire family to be there to help my father when he died. I began to make calls. I was able to contact everyone except my daughter Donna. I could not reach her until an hour later, when everyone else was already at the hospital. The dream had already told me what she would say: "It will take me at least an hour to get to the hospital."

We waited for her before removing life support.

This vision prepared me for my father's death. Although I was deeply saddened by his death, I realized that the gentle beauty of this dream was to make me understand that my father would soon be gone.

There are many cases like this one in *Parting Visions*. I found them intriguing, confirming, and comforting. It is clear from the documentation in this book that these spiritual experiences are with us far more than most of us will acknowledge.

For instance it is common for widows and widowers to have some kind of encounter with their departed loved one within a year of their death. The same is true for parents who lose children.

These visions are not frightening. Instead they are comforting events that help those who have them accept death. It is clear that visions can provide clarity at times of chaos, and renewal for a spirit that seems wrung out. As one woman in this book summed up so nicely, "When my [dead] mother appeared to me, I suddenly understood everything. I knew what would happen when I died and I knew what my goal on earth should be."

Visions and spiritual experiences happen frequently to those who are dying. Unfortunately these experiences are ignored or even ridiculed by many physicians. This is too bad, since they have great power to ease the dying process and heal grief in the living. In fact the healing benefits of these experiences are so great that, as Melvin Morse points out, if they were a pill, they would be prescribed in hospitals everywhere.

I have witnessed the power of these deathbed visions myself. Before the publication of *Embraced by the Light* I volunteered a lot of my free time to cancer patients. There I would sit with dying people, their bony arms wrapped around my neck, as they whispered to me about their deathbed visions.

I have less free time these days, but I still spend as much of it as I can with the dying.

I was giving a talk in New Orleans when I was contacted by a woman who begged me to spend time with her dying husband. He had been in a local hospital for several months with leukemia and was now at the end of his fight with that disease. He had read *Embraced by the Light* in preparation for death and had told his wife that his dying wish was to meet me. Would I come?

That evening I went to the hospital. The man I saw was clearly a shadow of his former self, a six-foot-two bag of bones and sallow skin.

He was too sick to get up, so we wheeled him in his bed to a window that overlooked the city. I dimmed the room lights, and we sat for a few moments in silence.

"What are your fears?" I asked him.

Tears flowed down his cheeks as he told me all of the mistakes he had made that kept him from being "a good Christian."

"God expects you to make mistakes," I said. "The Bible says 'to err is human.'"

He had been hanging on to life because he thought his wife was too weak to make it through life without him. In the past few months he had seen her gain strength as he wasted away. Now, he joked, she had become almost too strong. It was time to die.

Things had happened that confirmed it was time to die. Christ had come to him in a vision, reaching down from above and asking him to come with him.

The vision was real, just as real as the many others I had heard over the years. For him it was a signal that the end was now very near. It was reassuring for him to know that someone was going to be waiting for him when he died.

When I left this man, he had a comfort that no pill would have provided. His vision gave him hope for the future beyond this life and an understanding of the life that he was about to leave.

That is the nature of the death-related visions in this book.

They carry the power to heal, even when it seems to be past time for that.

This book is a leap forward in understanding death and the uses and meanings of death-related visions. It is clear to me that Melvin Morse has followed his spirit in researching this topic. Like many important medical researchers, he is being led in his work by faith, the subconscious knowledge that his work is beneficial to the body, mind, and spirit of mankind.

Being led by faith is far more difficult than being led by knowledge. Those of us who have had death-related visions and survived certainly applaud his work. We know he is on the right path.

PARTING VISIONS

1

VISIONS
AND REAL LIFE

—

In this light my spirit suddenly saw through all
. . . it knew God, who he is, and how he is and
what his will is.

—Jacob Boehme

"You have got to tell all the old people so that they won't be afraid to die!"

I nearly choked with emotions as the little boy before me spoke these words. I remembered when I first saw him. His name was Chris. It had been four years earlier when his limp body was brought to the hospital by helicopter. He had nearly drowned after his father lost control of the sedan he was driving and plunged over a bridge and into the freezing waters of a river near Seattle. His brother and mother were in the car too. All were dazed by the impact and stunned by the horror of sinking in the dark waters.

The impact had knocked the father unconscious. The mother was left to find a way out of the rapidly filling automobile. She unfastened her seatbelt and kicked at the passenger window. Nothing happened. Then, as she told me later, "I felt an indescribable sensation go through my body, and as this happened, I was given the physical strength to kick out the window." She did this despite three compression fractures sustained during impact.

Chris's mom, Patti, swam out through the passenger window, got to the surface, and grabbed the ski rack that was attached to the top of their car. Somehow, Chris's six-year-old brother, Johnny, had also gotten out of the car, and was floating down the river, unconscious. Johnny was almost out of reach before Patti was able to grab him and push him to the top of their car, which was about a foot underwater. The father and little Chris remained trapped inside. For a terrifying moment Chris struggled as the water enveloped him. Then he lost consciousness and "went to heaven." He was submerged in the icy water for almost fifteen minutes. As we spoke in the living room of his house, he told me again in his childlike way what that voyage was like.

"When I died, I went into a huge noodle," said Chris, who was four years old when the accident happened. "It wasn't like a spiral noodle, but it was very straight, like a tunnel. When I told my mom about nearly dying, I told her it was a noodle, but now I am thinking that it must have been a tunnel, because it had a rainbow in it, and I don't think a noodle has a rainbow.

"I was being pushed along by a wind, and I could kind of float. I saw two small tunnels in front of me. One of them was animal heaven and the other one was the human heaven. First I went into the animal heaven. There were lots of flowers and there was a bee. The bee was talking to me and we were both smelling flowers. The bee was very nice and brought me bread and honey because I was really hungry.

"Then I went to human heaven. I saw my grandmother [who had died years earlier]. Then I saw heaven. Human heaven was beautiful. It was like a castle, but not one of those grungy old places. This was not a golden castle, it was just a regular old castle. As I looked at heaven, I heard music. The music was very loud and it stuck in my head. I started looking around at it, and then all of a sudden I was in the hospital. Just like that I woke up, and there were nurses standing around me. It was just that easy."

I laughed when he got to the "easy" part. As I reviewed his case history, I could see that keeping him alive wasn't easy at all. He had been underwater over ten minutes until Dennis Johnson, a carpenter who had witnessed the accident, dove repeatedly to the sunken car and pulled the young boy from the backseat. He then towed Chris to shore and revived him with mouth-to-mouth resuscitation. "I know he was dead when I reached shore," said Johnson. "He wasn't breathing, but I had to try to bring him back to life anyway." This selfless act of heroism won Johnson a Carnegie Medal for Heroism and a Washington State Patrol Award of Merit, an honor usually reserved for state troopers. Chris was then airlifted to the nearest hospital, where further heroics were required to keep him alive.

Chris's father was the last one to be pulled from the car. He was airlifted to Harborview Hospital, where extensive efforts were made to resuscitate him. He died despite the efforts.

Now, four years later, Chris was sitting in the living room of his home casually playing what sounded like avant-garde jazz on a portable keyboard. His mother said he had shown little interest in music before the accident, but afterward she had to buy him a keyboard so that he could play the hauntingly beautiful tune he had heard while traveling through the "huge noodle."

I had been invited to hear Chris's story. An acquaintance of

Chris's mom was familiar with my work in near-death studies and thought that I would be interested in talking to her son about his experience at the threshold of death. Even though I have heard hundreds of children describe their near-death experiences, chills ran up my spine as I listened to Chris play the music of his experience. I taped the piece that Chris played and later had a professor of music listen to it. He said it sounded like an advanced piece of jazz being played by a child who had not yet developed the hand-eye coordination necessary to read music and play it. It sounded nothing like the kind of music I would associate with church or death.

I was deeply absorbed in the spiritual concert that was taking place.

Suddenly Chris stopped.

"I have to ask you a question," he said with the sophistication of someone ten years older. "How do I know that what happened was real? How do I know that I really went to heaven? How do I know that I wasn't just making it all up?"

REAL, NOT FANTASY

I had focused on that very question myself for ten years. From the day that I heard my first near-death experience and a little girl patted me on the hand and confidently told me, "You'll see, Dr. Morse, heaven is fun," I have sought to answer the very question that Chris was asking me.

I looked around the living room as everyone waited patiently for my response. Even with the years of research I have done on this topic, this is a difficult question for me to answer. I cleared my throat and smiled nervously at Chris.

"Chris, what happened to you is as real as it gets."

DIFFERENT EXPERIENCE, SAME QUESTION

"Dr. Morse, how do I know that what happened to *me* was real?"

This time the question didn't come from Chris but from his mother, Patti. She had asked me to come into the kitchen so that she could tell me in private what happened to her on that horrible night.

She began by saying that neither she nor her husband were religious people. They did not attend church, never prayed, and in fact did not believe in God. "My husband was a physicist and I was just a carefree ski instructor," she said. "We had a strong sense of family values, and were deeply in love, but never discussed spiritual matters."

On the night of the accident they were returning from the mountains, where Patti had been giving ski lessons to the children of a Seattle Seahawks football player. Her husband was driving too fast for the road conditions. Patti was telling him to slow down when he lost control and skidded off the bridge.

"After we hit the bottom of the river, I knew we had to get out. I unfastened my safety belt and kicked at the passenger window.

"After I broke the passenger window with my feet, I came to the surface of the water, gasping for air, and grabbed the ski rack. Out of the corner of my eye, I saw my six-year-old son, Johnny, floating down the river. I was barely able to reach him. I realized he wasn't breathing so I shook him with my free hand. Once I knew he was breathing again, I pushed him to the top of our car, and pulled myself up after him. I could feel the strong current of the river so I braced myself against the ski rack to keep us on the roof of the car, while holding Johnny's head out of the water, so that he could breathe.

"I started screaming for help, louder than I have ever screamed in my life. After several very long minutes, I saw the beam of a tiny flashlight, coming from downstream. Shortly thereafter, a man appeared, jumped in the water, and swam out to us. I started screaming about my baby being trapped in the car, and the man dove underwater several times, before coming to the surface with Chris."

Patti paused for a moment and then told me something she had not mentioned to any of the reporters who had interviewed her: "When I reached the surface of the water, I sensed that my husband was sitting on the rocks, watching the rescue below. It was eleven at night, pitch-dark and freezing cold, but there he was, sitting on the rocks."

Her husband seemed perfectly content to sit passively while others dove to save his son and himself. Patti became furious with her husband. "I was as angry as I have ever been with him," she said. "I began to scream at him, and when I did that, he disappeared."

Intellectually Patti felt that her husband was not on that rock. She knew that he was underwater, where rescuers were desperately trying to save him. Still the sensation was so intense that she will swear to this day that her husband had been sitting right there, watching the proceedings.

Soon after the accident, other visions began taking place. The first of these consisted of a number of intimate encounters with her deceased husband, when Patti was sleeping. However, she distinguished the things she experienced during these vivid encounters as different from her normal dream state. "It happened as I was waking up, but it was *not* a dream," she said. "It was too *real* to be a dream! I didn't want it to happen. It just happened."

In addition to this, Patti also claimed to have actually seen her deceased husband, at least two other times. On one of these occasions, she was wide awake, and sitting in her living room. She looked up and there he was, sitting on the couch. "He looked very normal. He was not transparent and he was wearing regular clothing."

At first she denied that these visions were anything but "a crazy widow thing." Then, about three weeks after the accident, Chris told her and his grandma about his experience of going to see his dead grandmother through the "huge noodle" and hearing the heavenly music. They listened in mute amazement as he told what had happened when he almost drowned. The effect on Patti was immediate.

"Suddenly it all came together for me," she said. "Before hearing his story I could only sleep for a few minutes without waking up in fear and terror. After hearing Chris's story I slept six hours and awoke fully rested."

"Why?" I asked.

"Because of Chris's experience I believe that my husband was letting me know that he was okay," she said. "Not that he was going to live, but that it was okay that he had died."

Was Patti's visionary experience "real"? She didn't wait for me to answer that question. Her son's near-death experience answered that question for her. When Chris told his mother about his experience, she accepted the visions of her husband as real events, not made-up dreams. In short, Chris's experience validated her own. She now believes in God and an afterlife, just as she accepts her husband's message to her that "everything is going to be all right," vague and nonspecific though that message might seem to an outside observer.

"My experience was as real as the one Chris had," said Patti. "And they have both given us such peace. How could I ever deny that they are real?"

Although she remains both confused and comforted by the various encounters involving her deceased husband, she has now grieved in a healthy manner. She feels strongly that her husband was telling her to live and love life rather than to dwell on the reasons for his premature death.

"We lost a lot in that accident," said Patti. "But the visions gave us depth, meaning, and the strength to carry on."

LIFE-CHANGING VISIONS

Patti's experience was similar to dozens of cases I have heard over the years. As I searched for near-death experiences to study, I would be approached by people who had had visions like Patti's, experiences that rocked them to their spiritual core and changed the very foundation of their life.

Since I was interested in visionary encounters, I would always listen to their stories and record them for further use, but I saw little connection between these visions and the field in which I was most interested at the time—the near-death experiences of little children.

Still these visions were interesting, productive, and sometimes quite intense. For example I was invited to speak about near-death experiences to a national meeting of critical-care nurses. Nurses are the perfect audience for this topic since they are far closer to patients than most doctors and therefore are more likely to talk about spiritual matters. Because of their proximity to patients, I wanted to make sure these nurses knew that visions are a normal part of the dying process and should be cherished, not feared. It was a simple message that sprang easily from the research I had done with children over the previous ten years.

After the talk one of the nurses was quite agitated. As I stood in the lobby talking to other nurses, I could see this woman bearing down on me through the crowd. She had an intensity in her eyes that made me think of an angry mother about to collar her badly behaved son. She came straight across the room, weaving around some of her fellow nurses and pushing others aside without uttering so much as "excuse me." She was heading for me, there was no doubt about that. I could feel my pulse rate climbing and my palms beginning to perspire. I knew that I had some explaining to do, I just didn't know about what.

"I read all of your papers in the medical journals," she stated. "How do you know these kids aren't just having a reaction to morphine or Valium?"

I calmly explained that I had researched patients who had been given large amounts of morphine and found that none of them had anything resembling a near-death experience.

"Okay, then, how do you know these kids just didn't invent the experience?" she demanded. "You know, critical-care patients sometimes tell amazing stories about monsters chasing them with needles. Maybe they are just making the whole thing up so that they can be on a talk show with the famous Dr. Morse."

The only thing that kept me from becoming angry at this point was the hurt that I saw in this woman's eyes. Although she seemed extremely angry, she was actually on the verge of tears as she spoke.

"The stories they tell aren't monster stories," I said. "They are amazingly consistent experiences that involve similar elements. And besides, I talked to most of these kids before I was the Dr. Morse of talk-show fame."

By this point in our conversation the nurse was shaking, and I could tell that something was genuinely bothering her. I led her to a bench and sat down with her. "What's wrong?" I asked. "Why is this so important to you?"

Tears sprang to her eyes as she told her story. When her daughter was fourteen, she came down with leukemia. The two vowed to fight this horrible illness with all the heart they could muster. During the next two years the girl was in the hospital for more than twenty weeks. "While other kids her age were worrying about dressing for the prom or how they looked in jeans, my daughter was wearing a wig and throwing up all day," said the nurse.

After her third relapse the oncologist took the mother aside and told her that her daughter was not going to live longer than a few more weeks.

"I wanted to have as much quality time with her as I could," the nurse told me. "In my heart I knew it was hopeless. The best gift I could give her would be to let her die in peace."

Unfortunately that didn't happen. As the daughter began to die, a team of doctors with life-support equipment began gathering in the room. The mother knew that any kind of life support was futile, as were any attempts at resuscitation. As a critical-care nurse she knew that her daughter was dying. Yet as a mother she found it impossible to tell the doctors to let the little girl die.

For several hours the doctors put lines into her arteries and tubes into her nose. When her heart stopped, they put paddles on her chest and shocked it back to life. When the mother gasped at what they were doing to her daughter, one of the assisting nurses escorted her into the hall and told her to wait there.

"Finally, when it was all over, they let me come back into the room," she said. "The entire resuscitation team streamed out with their heads hanging down because they had failed to keep her alive. They closed the door behind them, and I was left alone in the room with my daughter's body."

The mother sat there for quite some time in silence with her daughter's body. Then something shocking happened. The daughter sat up and looked her mother right in the eye! "She was alive, I know she was," said the mother. "She squeezed my hand and said, 'Don't worry, Mom, I'll be okay now.'"

She apologized to me for coming on so strong, but for the ten months since her daughter died, the nurse had dismissed this final visitation as being some sort of grief-induced hallucination.

"I wasn't out of my mind with grief," she told me. "I know what I saw as a nurse. But hearing your lecture, I realized my daughter could have come back for just a few seconds to give me that message. After hearing about near-death experiences I will never think about her death in the same way again."

INTRIGUING ENCOUNTERS

When I first heard this story I was skeptical. But intriguing stories like these kept popping up with great regularity. Sometimes the visions happened during periods of serious physical crisis, whereas at other times they happened during periods of personal crisis.

One such event happened to a doctor in San Francisco. She worked in the emergency room of a hospital on the bad side of the city. On a day-to-day basis she dealt with the worst society has to offer, from drug addicts with blood infections to children being beaten by their parents. Her life was so steeped in misery that she fell into a deep state of spiritual crisis in which she found herself unable to believe in God.

This loss of belief was very much on her mind on this particular day when she went hiking in the Sierras. The beauty of nature was so overwhelming that she felt as though she had to pray for the return of her faith. As she came upon a clearing, she fell to her knees and prayed from her heart. "Let me know that you exist. I must have a sign, or I will go crazy, I will lose my reason to live."

At that point another person rounded a bend in the trail and approached her. This was no ordinary hiker, this was a woman dressed entirely in white. She stopped in front of my friend and spoke her name. "Go with God," she said, and then went on her way.

My friend's reaction was certainly different from what mine would have been. My belief in God would have been firmly reinstated. Unfortunately for my friend her reaction was one of disbelief. She received no comfort at all from her vision and is still seeking answers to her spiritual questions. When she came to me with her story, her question was similar to the one Chris asked me: "Do you think that was really an angel, or do you think I just imagined the entire episode?"

I understand her feelings. After all, she lives in a society that would probably treat Jesus Christ, Martin Luther, and Muhammad with mind-numbing psychiatric drugs. Because of her medical training she could not trust a vision that affirmed the existence of a God who can communicate with us.

As I began to study the scientific literature on the subject of visions, I found it puzzling that we do not immediately accept and understand the significance of these events. I have found that death-related visions, for instance, are the most common paranormal events in our lives. So common are these visions that more than 10 percent of the population has had such a vision. The majority of parents whose children have died have visions of that child within a year of the death. These visions often bring about a lessening of grief for the parent. Despite the frequency of such visions most psychologists and grief counselors consider these experiences to be meaningless hallucinations. Many even go so far as to tell their patients that their visions mean nothing.

I think much of this is due to the language used to describe death-related visions. There are simply no adequate words in medical use to put a positive light on visionary experiences. As a result their power and meaning to people are misidentified.

The way in which this happens is illustrated quite well in the work of W. Dewi Rees, a physician who practiced in Wales in the 1950s. In 1971 he published research in the *British Medical Journal* dealing with visionary encounters of widows and widowers in a specific area of Wales. He reported that not only did the great majority of this study population have post-death contact with their dead spouses but some of these contacts extended over a period of twenty years. In addition young widowed people had visionary contact with the dead nearly as often as old people.

He concluded that the experiences were more common in people whose marriages were happy and in marriages with children. Rather than being disturbed by these encounters with the dead, the subjects were quite happy to have the company of their dead spouse. He even went on to point out that those who have such experiences are less likely to die in the year after the spouse's death than those who do not have them.

Even though Dr. Rees attributed obvious benefit to these visitations, he repeatedly described them as "hallucinations," a psychiatric term that implies pathology. It is precisely because we in medicine cannot help thinking of these events as hallucinations—abnormal functions of the mind—that many people consider themselves mentally ill for having visions. We don't even have words other than *hallucination* in the language of medicine to describe these experiences. That is why Chris's mother first referred to her experience as a "crazy widow thing."

Indeed most of us think of visions as "crazy widow things," fantasies of the mind brought about by derangements of brain chemistry. This belief persists despite the fact that every systematic study on death-related visions shows that they occur primarily in times of good physical and mental health and are rarely associated with fevers, medications, or dementia. Still the theory persists among scientists that these visions are simply the projections of a disordered mind.

AN EARLY CASE STUDY

Although deathbed visions can be found in the literature and lore of all ages, they were rarely mentioned in the scientific literature until the late 1920s, when they were studied by Sir

William Barrett, a physics professor at the Royal College of Science, in Dublin.

He would never have considered examining such a topic had it not been for an experience told to him by his wife, an obstetrical surgeon. On the night of January 12, 1924, she arrived home from the hospital eager to tell her husband about a case she had had that day.

She had been called into the operating room to deliver the child of a woman named Doris (her last name was withheld from the written account). Although the child was born healthy, Doris was dying from a hemorrhage. As the doctors waited helplessly next to the dying woman, she began to see things. As Lady Barrett tells it,

> Suddenly she looked eagerly towards part of the room, a radiant smile illuminating her whole countenance. "Oh, lovely, lovely," she said. I asked, "What is lovely?" "What I see," she replied in low, intense tones. "What do you see?" "Lovely brightness—wonderful beings." It is difficult to describe the sense of reality conveyed by her intense absorption in the vision. Then—seeming to focus her attention more intently on one place for a moment—she exclaimed, almost with a kind of joyous cry, "Why, it's Father! Oh, he's so glad I'm coming; he is so glad. It would be perfect if only W. [her husband] would come too."
>
> Her baby was brought for her to see. She looked at it with interest, and then said, "Do you think I ought to stay for baby's sake?" Then, turning toward the vision again, she said, "I can't—I can't stay; if you could see what I do, you would know I can't stay."

Although the story thus far was compelling, skeptics could still argue that it was nothing more than an hallucination due to lack of blood or triggered by fear of death. Indeed Sir William Barrett may have made that very point to his wife. Then he heard the rest of the story. It seems that the sister of Doris, Vida, had died only three weeks earlier. Since Doris was in such delicate condition, the death of her beloved sister was kept a secret from her. That is why the final part of her death-bed vision was so amazing to Barrett.

She spoke to her father, saying, "I am coming," turning at the same time to look at me, saying, "Oh, he is so near." On looking at the same place again, she said with a rather puzzled expression, "He has Vida with him," turning again to me saying, "Vida is with him." Then she said, "You do want me, Dad; I am coming."

This story was so inspirational to Barrett that he undertook a systematic study of deathbed visions. His was the first scientific study to conclude that the mind of the dying patient is often clear and rational. He also reported a number of cases in which medical personnel or relatives present shared the dying patient's vision.

The work of Sir William Barrett did not contribute to the theory that these visions were a form of wish fulfillment. In fact the deathbed vision often did not portray the type of afterlife the dying expected. For example Barrett reported several children who were disappointed to see angels with no wings. In one such case he described a dying girl who sat up suddenly in her bed and said, "Angels, I see angels." Then the girl was puzzled. "Why aren't they wearing wings?" If deathbed visions were simply a fantasy of the mind, says Barrett, why did this little girl see something different from her expectations?

JESUS WITH A HAT

I have documented similar cases that make the same point about wish fulfillment. In one such case a little girl who'd had a near-death experience said she saw Jesus. When I asked her what he looked like, she drew a picture of a man sitting on a log and wearing a red hat. He looked more like Santa Claus than Jesus. Yet hanging in her room was the classic picture of Jesus with long blond hair, a white robe, and Anglo-Saxon features. Had her vision been one of wish fulfillment, my guess is that she would have seen the version of Jesus that hangs over her bed.

ANGELS OF LIGHT

In my own research I have found angels to be an integral part of visions of all kinds. At least 50 percent of the children in my studies see "guardian angels" as a part of their near-death experience. I have also found that guardian angels lend their help at other times of crisis, when a person needs answers to bolster his or her flagging spirit.

Such experiences have been described by saints and religious leaders throughout history. In the Islamic religion, for instance, the Prophet Muhammad tells of being visited by three angels, who cleanse him. An angel spared Abraham's son from sacrifice, and one also spared Daniel from the lion's den. Saint Paul the Apostle spoke frequently in the Bible of coming in contact with angels. He also witnessed angels interacting with others. In one instance he claimed to have observed the souls of dead men being accompanied by angels, who protected them on their rise to heaven.

A *Time* magazine poll showed that 69 percent of Americans believe in the existence of angels. I have found many people who will readily admit that visionary experiences involving angels have made the world comprehensible to them and have given them the spiritual strength to press on.

One such account comes from a woman whose daughter was ill with leukemia. The girl was lucid when she became excited and began pointing to the end of her bed. The mother reported:

I asked her what she saw, and she said that there was a boy at the end of the bed. She was not frightened by this boy. She was really quite glad to see him. Over the next couple of days she carried on conversations with him and was glad to have him there. With everything that was going on, it was almost as though this little boy that only she could see was stability for her. I think he was an angel.

In another instance a twelve-year-old girl tried to commit suicide by shooting herself in the face with a shotgun. She was nearly successful and was since operated on several times to reverse the damage done by the blast.

She reported that as she lay in her bedroom dying, a "seven-foot man" came in and told her that she would be all right. She could tell "by the way he held himself" that she had done something wrong in attempting suicide. "But he stayed with me all day until I got out of my first surgery," she said. "I haven't seen him since then, but I know he is still around me all the time."

Angels are reported under a variety of circumstances. Another account comes from Dr. Frank Oski, a professor of pediatrics under whom I trained at Johns Hopkins University. Oski is not a new-age guru. Rather he is a demanding pediatrician with an encyclopedic knowledge of medicine who insisted that his students come to the hospital having read the latest medical-journal articles. Yet to my great surprise Dr. Oski has been touched by the same mystical light described by people down through the ages who have had visions, including near-death experiences.

As a medical student Oski was enthusiastic about the potential of modern medicine, but frustrated by the fact that children die of congenital defects that are beyond anyone's control. One night he went to bed pondering the fate of a dying patient. Although he was doing his best, the child was not improving. He felt powerless to help and went to sleep wondering why this child had to die.

About an hour after falling asleep Oski was awakened by a bright light, one that shone in his room like a private sun. Oski could make out the form of a woman in the glow of the intense light. She had wings on her back and was approximately twenty years old.

In a quiet and reassuring voice the woman explained to the speechless Oski why it was that children had to die.

"The angel (I don't know what else to call her) said that life is an endless cycle of improvements and that humans are not perfect yet. She said that most people have this secret revealed to them when they die, but that handicapped children often know this and endure their problems without complaining because they know that their burdens will pass. Some of these children, she said, have even been given the challenge of teaching the rest of us how to love.

" 'It stretches our own humanity to love a child who is less than perfect,' said the angel. 'And that is an important lesson for us.' "

Oski has been courageous enough to talk freely about his experience. He has even written about it for a major pediatric journal. In that article he wrote, "I will make no attempt to convince you as to the reality of my story. But I would merely ask that you keep an open mind on the mysteries of life which occur to you on a daily basis."

SHARED VISIONS

Although they seem vividly real, visions like Oski's could be dismissed as being just vivid dreams and nothing more. I might be inclined to dismiss some of these experiences as dreams, too, if it were not for the similarity of these experiences to visions that happen to people who are clearly awake.

The reality of these visions becomes more convincing when they happen to a number of people at the same time.

I call these shared visions. I have heard a number of these and verified most of them. Perhaps the most amazing of these visions is the case of Olga Gearhardt, of San Diego, California.

Olga is the matriarch of a large and tight-knit family that includes four children, several grandchildren, and a number of relatives in California, Arizona, and New Mexico.

In 1988 a virus attacked Olga's heart and destroyed much of the muscle. Her heart became so weak that it could no longer beat effectively. The only chance she had for survival was a heart transplant.

Olga was put on the transplant-recipient list at the University of California Medical Center. People who are on this list must be in constant contact with the hospital where the transplant will be done. If a heart becomes available that matches their blood type, it must be implanted within hours of the donor's death for the transplant to be effective.

Olga's entire family was notified of this fact, and they all promised to lend moral support by being there at the hospital during her surgery. Early in 1989 Olga received the call from the hospital that a matching heart had been found. As she and her husband left for the hospital, her children started a telephone chain that notified family members in three states that the transplant was about to begin. In a matter of hours the waiting room of the hospital was overloaded with Olga's family.

The only member of the family not at the hospital was Olga's son-in-law. Although he loved his mother-in-law, he had a phobia about hospitals and preferred to await the news at home.

Late that evening her chest was opened and the transplant was performed successfully. At two-fifteen A.M. she developed unexpected complications, and the new heart would not beat properly. As the medical personnel became alarmed, the heart suddenly stopped beating altogether. It took several hours of resuscitation before the heart finally began functioning properly. Meanwhile the family in the waiting room was told nothing about these complications, and most of them were asleep. About six in the morning the family was told that the operation was a success but that she had almost died when the new heart failed.

Olga's daughter immediately called her husband to tell him the good news. "I know she's okay," he said. "She already told me herself."

He had awakened at two-fifteen to see his mother-in-law standing at the foot of his bed. It was as though she was standing right there, he said. Thinking she had not had surgery and had somehow come to his house instead, he sat up and asked her how she was.

"I am fine, I'm going to be all right," she said. "There is nothing for any of you to worry about." Then she disappeared.

The vision didn't frighten the son-in-law, but he did get out of bed and write down the time she appeared to him and exactly what was said.

When the family went in to see her, Olga began talking about "the strange dream" that took place during surgery. She said she had left her body and watched the doctors work on her for a few minutes. Then she went into the waiting room, where she saw her family. Frustrated by her inability to communicate with them, she decided to travel to her daughter's home, about thirty miles away, and connect with her son-in-law.

She told them that she was sure she had stood at the foot of her son-in-law's bed and told him that everything was going to be all right.

There is no way to dismiss this story as an hallucination or as a phenomenon of a chemically imbalanced brain. One could accuse Olga and her family of fraud, but my coauthor and I have devoted considerable time to investigating this story, interviewing several members of the family. We have found no discrepancies in any of their stories and no motive to invent such a story.

The only explanation is this: During the time this woman was on a heart-lung machine because her new heart was not functioning properly, she was able to leave her body and communicate with her son-in-law, who was in bed more than thirty miles away.

"CHRISSY CAME TO HELP ME"

A story similar to Olga's is documented by a doctor at the Enarby Vancouver General Hospital, in Vancouver, British Columbia.

He tells of two young cancer patients who had spent time together in the hospital's oncology ward. The two girls—Sandra and Chrissy—were together for several weeks as the doctors tried chemotherapy treatments to stop the cancers that plagued them. Finally Sandra was sent home to die, hundreds of miles away from Chrissy. The children had no contact with each other, nor did the families.

Months later Sandra became so ill that she sank into a deep coma. After a few hours she regained consciousness with a relieved look on her face. "Mommy, I went to heaven, and Chrissy came to help me," she said. "She told me I shouldn't be afraid because she was there to help me in heaven."

After this vision Sandra had no fear of her impending death. She described heaven as a place of beautiful white light and said that she would be glad to have a friend like Chrissy there with her.

It wasn't until days after Sandra had died that her mother and father discovered that Chrissy had died several weeks before their daughter.

For the parents of both children Sandra's deathbed vision was a relief. They now felt that the two girls were together in heaven.

RESPONSIBILITY TO RESEARCH

We tend all too often to trivialize these experiences by calling them dreams and fantasies caused by some kind of mental derangement. I frequently receive phone calls at home from my fellow physicians who encounter these experiences and are puzzled by them. Sometimes they are experiences that have happened to patients, and other times they are deeply personal.

One physician told me a sad story in which she felt her spirit being drawn together with that of her dying son. She said they entered a heavenly place together and then she let the boy go. Now she draws tremendous comfort from this experience and feels that she has firsthand knowledge that her son is in a "heavenly world."

Nevertheless she has been reluctant to go public with her story. As she put it, "Mel, when they start burning witches again, I want them to come for you first."

By this she meant that we often have irrational fear and prejudice of anything that is of a spiritual nature. Challenging such fears can be damaging to one's career. Yet for me the very reason I became a physician seemed to be at stake. My role as a physician is to understand the complete human being, and frankly there is no deeper expression of humanity than spiritual experience.

With my interest in the visionary experience piqued, I realized that my responsibility was to examine visionary experiences scientifically in order to help forge a new understanding of the divine.

I began by examining dozens of cases my research team had

collected. We looked at a wide variety of visionary experiences, from near-death experiences and deathbed visions to vivid dreams and spontaneous experiences of mystical light. It soon became clear to me that the near-death experience that happened to Chris when he almost drowned was very similar to the visionary experience of Dr. Oski.

If we could show that there is a common thread that runs throughout all these visions, I thought, then we would be able to shine light on the source of mysticism, one of mankind's greatest mysteries.

2

IN A NEW
LIGHT

—

Descriptions of people are not just poetic,
but a needed part of science, too.

—Oliver Sacks

I decided to focus on death-related visions.

Death-related visions are probably the least controversial of all paranormal experiences. They have been amply reported in popular books and scientific journals, and most physicians at least accept that they take place. Their meaning, however, is what is controversial.

Most scientists regard these visions as vivid hallucinations, factoids of the brain. For this reason few serious attempts have been made to integrate them into the grieving process itself. It is now obvious to me that these visions have tremendous power to heal or create guilt, depending upon how they are used and perceived by the person who has them. For widows who have such spiritual visions, they are a comforting vision of their lost husband. For parents whose child dies after they had a dream that foretold the death, a pre-death vision can be a source of anguish if they feel guilty that they did not act on the premonition.

In the course of researching visionary experiences I encountered the entire spectrum of reactions, from relief and joy to grief and anguish. I realized that these visions are not just hallucinations or wishful thinking but useful events that can make powerful changes in the life of the person who has them.

The visionary experiences I found in the course of my research proved to be anything but fantasies of the mind. Rather they were paranormal experiences that framed real events.

Let's start with Lila Morgan's vision.

"HE'S GOING TO BE WITH ME"

Lila Morgan grew up as the only child of Rick Dress, a professional baseball player whose last job was coaching for the New York Mets, when he died unexpectedly of a heart attack in 1963. She has fond memories of baseball and its players and tells funny stories about her grandmother flirting with the great Yankee first baseman Lou Gehrig when he came to their house for a visit.

She was close to her father and learned by his example how to be successful in a tough, male-dominated world. She lives by the precepts that made her father a successful athlete: "Work hard, do your best, pursue everything, and if an opportunity arises or a door opens, don't ignore it." By following that advice she has become the successful owner of a Los Angeles public relations firm and is the executive director for fund-raising for the Lou Gehrig's Disease Foundation in Los Angeles.

Currently she is director of development for the Association for Retarded Citizens in Southeast Los Angeles County.

In 1962 Lila's father went to his doctor for a complete checkup. He had been bothered by indigestion and wanted to make sure that no stomach problems were developing. Later that day he was told by the doctor that all the tests came back normal.

At about three in the morning Lila awoke from a deep sleep to find her room filled with an opaque white light. As she tells it,

I could never explain it. I paint oil paintings, and I could never paint it either. The room filled with this light and I heard a soothing voice say, "I'm going to take him."

The voice said it over and over again until I said, "Did he do anything wrong?"

"Oh, no," said the voice. "He is going to be with me."

Even though Lila describes the voice as being "filled with love," she sat up in bed feeling "as cold as death" and looked at the clock pointing at three A.M. For a while she thought that the voice was talking about her husband, who was now rubbing her arms, trying to warm her up. Then the telephone rang. It was her grandmother calling to tell her that her father had died unexpectedly at approximately three-fifteen A.M.

"I hate to say this, but I felt so good," said Lila. "I felt wonderful, I felt at peace. 'Don't worry,' I told my grandmother. 'I know it's okay.' "

As Lila tells it, "My dream saved my life. I was an only child and I lived for my father. I even looked like him. If this hadn't taken place, I would have been devastated."

For Lila this was no dream. It had such a vivid dimension that she can only qualify it as a vision. "I know now for sure that a soul lives on after death," she told me. "It was a relief to hear someone say that he was going to care for my father."

"SHE WAS ABSOLUTELY AFLAME"

For the most part these visions are comforting to the people who have them. If nothing else people are soothed by the fore-knowledge that a death has occurred. "If we are told that it's going to happen by a spirit, then doesn't that prove an after-life?"

That hypothesis came from a man I'll call George, a retiree in Arizona, who saw a comforting vision of his daughter as she died unexpectedly more than a thousand miles away. I'll quote George in full so that you can see how such an experience unfolds:

Our daughter had breast cancer for about two years before she died. It had spread to the bone, and the doctors were doing the best they could to stop it. She had had surgery and radiation and chemotherapy and was doing pretty well.

In June of that year we flew to Michigan to see her. We could see that the cancer treatment had been tough on her. She had lost too much weight and didn't have but an ounce of energy. She said that was normal, that the phase of treatment she was in left her weak. She was sure that she would come out of it in the next few weeks.

I have prostate cancer myself, so we talked a lot about how mentally and physically draining it can be. We even tried to joke about our diseases. "Like father, like daughter," I said. It helped to have the gallows humor, but there was no doubt in my mind that she was afraid of her disease.

At the end of June my wife and I flew back to Arizona. We made plans to see one another again in the fall. There was no indication that this wouldn't be the case. We spoke on the telephone several times after that, and she said that she was actually feeling better.

Anyway, July fifteenth is when the dream took place. I wasn't feeling well and had gone to bed early that night. About an hour later my wife came to bed, too, and I woke up when she got under the covers. That was at ten-thirty. Right around midnight I had a funny feeling inside of me, a kind of nervous stirring. I opened my eyes, and there at the foot of the bed was my daughter. She was glowing so bright that it was as though she was absolutely aflame.

I just looked at her a few moments and then I said, "Bonnie, what's going on?" When I sat up to look at her, she disappeared.

By this time my wife was awake. She saw me sitting up and asked what was wrong. Without a moment's hesitation I said, "Bonnie is dead." Just like that. Somehow I knew that the vision meant she was gone.

George immediately called his daughter's home in Michigan and spoke to a neighbor lady, who had been called by Bonnie's husband to baby-sit their kids. She tearfully told George that Bonnie had had a fatal reaction to the chemotherapy and had died at the hospital within the last hour.

"The vision took the edge off our grief," said George. "We were deeply broken up by our daughter's death, but through it all the vision gave us a distinct sense of awe and wonder about living and dying."

A SOURCE OF NEW OPINIONS

I was beginning to form new opinions about both visions and near-death experiences. I began to realize that there was a host of visions cut from the same cloth. Here are two more case studies that led me in this new direction.

I'll call the man in this first case David. He is a lieutenant in the fire department of a major city. His clipped tone and use of medical jargon revealed years of experience. Yet underneath the professional veneer I could hear the quavering voice of a man whose worldview had been shaken. "I haven't told anybody else about this," he said to me when we met. "I could only tell you because others might doubt my sanity. I just know that what happened to me was real."

Here is David's story:

I went to bed as usual on Sunday night; there was nothing different at all. But after being asleep for a couple of hours I had an extremely vivid dream about my brother. He was just sitting there in the living room, and everything seemed completely normal. Then I suddenly had the feeling that he was dead. I began to panic, but he just laughed.

"Don't worry," he said. "There's nothing to be worried about."

"I'm not worried," I said. "Why should I worry? You're not dead."

I got no reply from him when I said that. He just remained seated in the living room while I got more and more worried.

David awoke covered with sweat. He thought that maybe all the tragedy he had seen in the course of his job had finally gone to his head. He thought about calling his brother's house but realized that a call at such a late hour would not sit well with his brother or his family. After staying awake for several hours he finally fell back to sleep.

"Early in the morning I got a call from my sister-in-law," said David. "She told me that my brother had been killed in a head-on collision in a car with a drunk driver."

"GOOD-BYE, THANK YOU"

Without a doubt these visionary experiences are often disturbing to the person who has them. "Am I crazy?" they ask. Or, "Do normal people see things like this?" They often tell no one about their visions and only come to me because I am a physician who openly investigates such things. Yet in almost all of these cases there has been a comfort factor as well. As I've heard more and more stories, it has become clear to me that there is a spiritual side to humankind that has been forgotten or dismissed as unimportant or not "real." This side affirms the deep spiritual intuitions of religious leaders and ordinary people and holds a secret that can heal.

Few case studies illustrate the healing aspect of these visions so well as that of a nurse I'll call Mary.

Mary was a veteran nurse at a major university hospital. By her own admission she had "seen it all." She had worked in all the wards, from pediatrics to oncology, and was beyond being surprised or shocked by anything she might see in a hospital.

In her own life she faced the painful reality that her mother was dying of stomach cancer. Mary knew the score and talked openly with her mother about her chances of survival. "You could live another ten years or another ten months," she told her mother. "It all depends on what course the cancer takes in your body."

Mary moved her mother into her own home. There she became worse and worse, one time actually sinking into a coma that Mary thought marked the end, but still her mother survived.

Meanwhile Mary left her job and devoted her life to her mother's care. She changed her diapers, cooked her meals, and washed her body. As her mother wasted away, she became more distant and finally didn't respond to Mary's presence at all.

One morning Mary walked into her mother's bedroom to find her smiling and staring at the foot of the bed. Mary was elated. She took her mother's coherence and smile to be an early sign of recovery. She thought that her long vigil had not been in vain.

A few minutes later Mary was humming to herself in the laundry room when she felt a chill and a puff of wind brush her hair. "Good-bye, thank you," she thought she heard her mother whisper.

Mary rushed down the hall and into her mother's room and found her dead. Mary's world suddenly turned upside down. She had thought recovery was possible, but now she felt as though she had been kicked in the stomach. All of her hard work had been for naught, she told me. Now she felt as though she should have taken everybody's advice and let her mother die in the hospital. It certainly would have been less emotionally draining than what she had been through.

Her mother smiling and staring at the end of the bed, the puff of wind, and the final farewell that led her to run back into her mother's bedroom were things that she dismissed as some sort of weird fantasy. Her extensive medical training made her disbelieve this very real experience.

Mary remained bitter about her mother's death for some time. Then she happened to read my research on near-death experiences in the pediatric journals published by the American Medical Association. In those articles I presented research to make the point that near-death experiences happen at the point of death and are not "made up" later to soothe a person's fear of having nearly died. That simple fact alone makes them "real" events, at least as real as the world we see around us.

Mary made a logical connection that I had not made myself. If near-death experiences are real, then so too are a variety of other death-related experiences. Suddenly she saw her own experience in a different light. Rather than thinking of herself as being crazy, she realized that her mother had actually thanked her and said good-bye. And rather than dismissing the time she spent with her mother as having been wasted, she now sees it as the most spiritually affirming time of her life.

This nurse made a connection that I had not made myself: Near-death experiences validate an entire host of death-related visions. These visions have the power to quell our fear of dying and to heal our grief.

I began to take seriously the notion that near-death experiences come from the same source as visionary encounters, as well as pre- and post-death visitations and even certain dreams. I also believed that with a little work I could distinguish a true vision from hallucinations and other pathological brain processes, such as lack of oxygen.

GATHERING STORIES

Science is not simply the collection of stories. Rather it is the development of testable hypotheses. Without those hypotheses my research would be published in the *National Enquirer* instead of prestigious medical journals. In order to arrive at these conclusions we have to collect and examine the stories of people who have had these visionary experiences.

We arrive at truths by listening to patients. Sometimes what they tell us cannot be reproduced immediately at will or replicated in the lab, but they are truths nonetheless.

More and more scientists are realizing this, which is why a new science has sprung up over the last twenty years known as qualitative data analysis. This is the science of interpreting information obtained from other human beings in the field rather than in a laboratory setting. This method takes into consideration the fact that people are not lab rats and are continuously subject to a number of variables.

Qualitative research is becoming the mainstay of science in such areas as nursing, psychology, anthropology, political science, and, yes, medicine. Through the qualitative sciences we have been able to help people stop smoking, lose weight, and gain an understanding of spiritual experiences. This type of research is a source of rich descriptions and explanations of mental processes. It is what Albert Einstein was talking about when he said, "The whole of science is nothing more than a refinement of everyday thinking."

For my early work in this field I relied upon case studies of death-related visions I had collected for my research on near-death experiences. While I was researching that topic, many people came to me with their own stories about visionary encounters with departed loved ones, or vivid dreams that were precognitive. I could not use these cases in my near-death-experience research because the people who experienced them were never near death. Still I hung on to the raw data, intuitively thinking that there was a link between these events and near-death experiences. Somewhere, I thought, there is a direct connection between all death-related visions.

As I examined the cases, I began to realize that visionary experiences are very similar to near-death experiences. Indeed what are often called in medical textbooks grief-induced hallucinations are not hallucinations at all but normal brain processes that happen to be visionary. Here is an example from a California woman I'll call Carla.

"YOU WILL NOT DIE, CARLA"

At the age of twenty she had been bothered by bone pain, and X rays and other tests revealed that she had a tumor. Plans were made to biopsy the tumor to see what kind of cancer it was. On the day Carla was taken into surgery, she was extremely nervous. Besides the anxiety of surgery, hers could only be bad news or worse news. After all, the operation was to find out what kind of cancer she had, not whether or not she had it.

In the middle of the surgery, while under anesthesia, she had the vision. She suddenly became aware of a light approaching her and filling her body. As that happened, a voice said to her, "You will not die, Carla, you will live at least forty-five more years. Do not be afraid to live or die."

Her tumor proved to be Ewing's sarcoma, an extremely aggressive tumor from which few recover. Such cancers rarely respond to treatment of any kind. Most patients who have it die within a few years of being diagnosed. Carla's was different. Her tumor responded to treatment immediately and eventually disappeared altogether.

I am certainly not suggesting that the spiritual light cured her tumor. Carla doesn't even know herself if she thinks this is true. It may simply be that her tumor was going to remit on its own and the being of light was there to let her know this.

Although visions do not necessarily occur in a cause-and-effect manner, many do. As you can see from the following case studies, visions frequently appear during periods of crisis. When they do, they provide a special form of help and comfort.

CASE I:
"YOU ARE NOT TO DIE LIKE THIS"

Mebruke is a thirty-year-old Saudi Arabian living in New York City. At the age of twenty she was swimming in the Mediterranean Sea off the coast of Italy when she became tired. As she headed for shore, she realized that she was too far out to make it back. She began to struggle and swallow water. Finally she slipped beneath the waves.

I went under for the fourth time, and my body went limp and I wasn't aware of it anymore. It was at this point that I saw a beautiful white light. It was so bright and yet it had such a calming effect that the more I looked at it, the calmer I felt. To this day I can't really say

*what that light was. In my religion [Muslim] there are beings called
angels who are made out of pure white light. Maybe that is what I
saw.*

*Anyway, while I was underwater, I heard a voice say, "You are not
to die like this." Suddenly I felt this energy shoot through me from my
feet to my head, and at the same time I seemed to be propelled out
of the water. It was as if someone was physically bringing me out of
the water, but I can swear that there was no physical being there.*

*I was moved through the water, I don't know how else to describe
it. Before long a boat came, and a man reached over the side and
pulled me out. When he did that, I started to laugh because I was so
glad to be out of the water.*

This intense vision was associated with the woman surviving
a near-fatal event, although she was technically not near death.
We cannot hope to understand NDEs unless we can understand this experience as well.

CASE 2:
"I WENT WITH YOU TO SEE BABY SISTER"

A vision with a twist occurred to a woman I'll call Diedra. As a
mother of a healthy five-year-old girl, she was happy to discover
that she was pregnant again. The baby inside of her seemed
healthy too. During all the prenatal visits the fetus had a strong
heartbeat and seemed to be quite normal. Toward the end of
her pregnancy she was delighted to be able to see her child
with ultrasound and to know that she would soon be holding
her.

But when the baby was born, her lungs were not fully developed, and she died from not being able to breathe air. The death was a blow to Diedra:

I was in shock for weeks afterward. I had a six-year-old girl and I couldn't even hug her or cry in front of her. I didn't take care of myself, and I would go to the graveyard alone, sometimes at night, and just sit and cry. I thought I was going to go crazy and I can say now that I really wanted to die. I didn't care about anything anymore, not even my husband or daughter.

Then one night I was at the graveside. It was a warm summer night, but all of a sudden I became very cold. When I looked around, it wasn't dark anymore, it was sunny. I know this sounds mad, but I felt myself being pulled up a tunnel of light.

At the end of this tunnel I found myself sitting on a hill watching adults play with children. I watched one of these adults playing with a child that I knew was my baby. I watched this for some time and then I faded back to darkness, where I was sitting there at her graveside.

The experience seemed so real to Diedra that she could hardly keep from telling her husband what had happened. If she told him, she knew that he would think she was mentally disturbed and would have her examined by a psychiatrist.

Instead of telling anyone, she sat down at the dining-room table and began reading the newspaper. It was then that the twist occurred. Her six-year-old daughter approached her with a huge smile on her face. "Mommy," she said. "I went with you to see baby sister. She's dead now, isn't she? Next time give her a hug for me. I miss her."

There is no doubt in this woman's mind that her daughter shared the vision of her lost child. Not only did this vision help her return to what she had and put the death behind her, it also gave her relief in feeling that her child was being cared for in a heavenly realm. This experience has the elements of the NDE, including the tunnel and the light. But again, it did not occur in the context of near death.

CASE 3:
"I NOW HAD THE COURAGE TO RETURN HOME"

One of the greatest challenges of mourning is adapting to life without the departed loved one. The house remains a sort of sad shrine to the person, a place in which objects are never moved in a desperate attempt to stop time. Sometimes people cannot even bear to stay in the same house.

That was the case with Mabel. After thirty years of marriage and six children, her husband died, leaving her a rich but mourning widow.

She traveled all over the world and spent more time with her children than was sometimes comfortable. Her goal was simply to keep moving and to stay away from the house where her husband had died. "It was just too sad a place for me to be," she said, explaining her constant need to travel.

This all changed one night when she happened to be in town between trips. She was sleeping in the bed that she and her husband had slept in for years when she was awakened by a noise in the backyard.

I thought there was a noisy dog in our backyard or something. I got up and went downstairs and then went out onto the porch overlooking the backyard. There I saw a turtle walking across the grass. This turtle looked at me almost the way a human would. Then it just changed into a white dove and flew away.

This vision was one of the most interesting to me. Even though her husband didn't present himself in the usual form, she saw great symbolic meaning in what did happen. This dream left her with the unmistakable impression that life changes. She interpreted her vision to mean that she had been living like a turtle and should now feel free to come and go as she liked.

"I now felt that the house was free of him and he of it," she said. "I had the courage to return home." This experience is similar to the NDE in its vividly real quality.

CASE 4:
"IT WAS A MIRACLE"

Norma is a lively seventy-three-year-old woman who let me know right away that she was glad—and lucky—to be alive. She has survived two major surgeries—brain and open-heart surgery. A visionary experience that happened minutes before her brain surgery convinced her that she still had a long life ahead of her.

My experience with the brain tumor took place in 1943. At that time they knew very little about what to do with brain tumors. Since then I have heard this time referred to as the Dark Ages of brain surgery, because they didn't have nearly the number of techniques that they do now.

I had been diagnosed with a brain tumor and was scheduled for surgery. I had two children and I was as scared for them as I was for myself, because I was sure I was going to die, if not from the operation, then from brain cancer later on.

Anyway, my husband was pushing me down the aisle in a wheel-

chair. I was going to my room the night before surgery and I was crying my eyes out. All of a sudden I had the most wonderful feeling pass over me, and a voice said, "Don't cry, you're going to be all right."

Right away I stopped crying. I turned to my husband and told him what I had just heard. After that I wasn't afraid anymore. They took the tumor out, and nothing more ever came of it.

Norma calls these words of encouragement a miracle. When she was in her sixties, she had to have open-heart surgery. Rather than crying this time, she calmly underwent the surgery. "I knew once again that it wasn't my time yet," she said.

A STUDY OF DREAMERS

Without a doubt the case studies we were gathering were intriguing, but the skeptic inside of me had some questions as well. What sort of dreams do people have that *don't* come true?

Perhaps everyone has a vivid visionary dream occasionally. In a country of 280 million people it is not surprising that a person might have a dream that coincidentally comes true. Or maybe people have dreams of dread all the time and only remember the ones that seem to be linked to dramatic events in their lives, like recovery from illness. This is what is known as recall bias. Could all of these visionary dreams I was collecting just be examples of selective recall?

To get the answers I needed, I turned to my own pediatrics practice. I decided to study the parents of my patients, asking two hundred of them to record every sort of dream or vision they had for the next two years. This included a wide range of

people, from aircraft engineers to welfare mothers, from restaurant owners to Vietnamese refugees.

I had them answer a simple questionnaire in which they
were asked such questions as:

- Have you ever had a vivid premonition that something terrible has happened or will happen to someone close to you and
then nothing of the sort happened?
- Have you ever had a feeling or dream or vision that your
child or spouse was going to die soon, and then it did not happen?
- Have you ever had the intuition or impression that something was going to happen, for example a car accident, and
then the event did not happen?

The point of asking them for dreams and premonitions that
did *not* come true was to compare the quality of those experiences with the ones from my previous studies that had come
true. I wanted to see what traits the precognitive experiences
had that were not present in the experiences that did not come
true.

DREAMS THAT COME TRUE

By analyzing the results from this study and comparing my
findings to the visionary case studies, I realized I had made an
exciting discovery. When comparing these ordinary dreams
with ones that had a quality of reality or were actually precognitive, I found that it was possible to reliably predict which
dreams were likely to be followed by real events. I did this by

deconstructing the dreamlike visions and then looking for common elements that made up a core experience. I found that visionary dreams have at least two of the following elements:

■ A "Real" or "Hyperreal" Quality. Psychical dreams frequently convey the sense of absolute reality. They are often described as being "unlike any dream I have ever had before." For instance a woman who had had a visitation from a "guardian angel" after her husband died described the glowing woman who came into her room as being "just like a person standing there. I am sure I could have gone right up and touched her."

■ Sights and Sounds That Are Superimposed Over Ordinary Reality. A great example of this comes from a woman in Seattle who had a vivid dream about her father dying suddenly, which he did about six days later. She was so shaken by the dream that she felt a need to sit up for a while until her anxiety passed. When she did, she found herself walking through a mist that was rising from the floor. When she turned her bedroom light on, the mist disappeared.

This sort of image superimposed over reality is common in visionary experiences. It can include such things as a voice that warns of impending danger or the vision of a spirit before a crowd.

■ A Unique Character to the Dream That Is Unlike Anything Experienced Before. Most dreams go unremembered, but the visionary encounters in my study were so vivid that they could not be forgotten. As one person described it, "My vision stuck in my mind more deeply than my last vacation. I think about it all the time, especially when I need to realize that there is more to life than my own little reality."

■ *Coherent and Useful Information That Has Meaning for Other People as Well as for the Dreamer.* Even if a visionary dream is a metaphor for something else, its meaning can be clearly understood when its contents are described to someone else. This is what distinguishes true experiences from psychotic visions. One of the best examples of this does not come from my study but from the case of James Chaffin, who died in North Carolina in 1921.

Chaffin's formal will, written fifteen years before his death, bequeathed all of his property to his third son, leaving out his wife and two other sons.

Why he favored one son over everyone else in his family isn't known, but his spirit obviously wasn't at rest with it. Four years later his second son had a visitation from his father during a dream. "My will is in my overcoat pocket," he said.

He told his dream to his older brother, and the two searched their father's old clothing and found a note sewn into the lining of his overcoat. The note said, "Read the twenty-seventh chapter of Genesis in my daddy's old Bible."

In the presence of witnesses the Bible was opened, and a handwritten will was discovered that was dated 1919. The courts investigated the case for fraud and found none. The new will was honored, which called for the estate to be divided equally among the living family members.

■ *A Mystical White Light or a Spiritual Being of Light.* As far as I am concerned, an experience of light is the hallmark of a very deep experience. I have studied people who have had mystical visions of light and found that they were as greatly transformed by their experience as those who had had near-death experiences.

An example of this comes from a man whose brother died in an airplane crash in the southern United States. Several days after the crash the man and his father visited the crash site. The crash had been picked clean by forensic crash specialists, and white chalk marks outlined the places where bodies had been found.

Suddenly a metal object captured the attention of both men. The father picked it up only to find that it was his dead son's identification bracelet. Both men reported a sudden flash of light that lingered. Both had feelings of great relief after this. They had both been greatly disturbed by his death, but after the experience of the light they accepted it and had a deep sense of inner peace.

AFFIRMING CONCLUSIONS

Without shared experiences, in which two or more people have the same visionary encounter, skeptics could build a good case that visionary experiences are created by the mind. But shared experiences all but close the door on that theory. They imply that our minds are capable of reaching out and communicating with other minds in an extrasensory way. Some of them even suggest that there is a part of the human brain that allows us to access another reality, one in which we gain fundamental insights into our lives.

Wilder Penfield, the father of modern neuroscience, documented the fact that we have such an area in the right temporal lobe of the brain. I call it the " 'out of body' and 'see God' " area.

I think this area is as much a part of a normal brain as are those parts that allow us to control our arms and legs. And just like those specialized areas, it can be accessed in a variety of ways. By that I mean that people who have visions or prophetic dreams are using the same area of the brain as that used during near-death experiences. In fact, these "circuit boards of mysticism" can be triggered in many ways, from childbirth to physical abuse to nearly dying.

How it works is more complex than it might seem. For instance, what is it that allows this area to receive information from outside the body, which is the only way that many of the visions discussed in this chapter and other psychic experiences can be explained? How is it that a woman carrying a baby with Down's syndrome or heart disease knows her baby has a birth defect long before medical tests confirm it? These are questions that make me wonder if there isn't more to this area of the brain than ordinary gray matter.

"WE BOTH SAW THE MEN"

I think that the strongest indication that some external communication is taking place comes from those rare times when a near-death experience or vision is simultaneously shared with another person. Such a sharing represents the ultimate activation of our "circuit boards of mysticism."

For instance, a woman I'll call Carol told me of a vision she shared with her husband, a vision of light that seemed to heal her chronic ailment.

By the time I turned fifty, I had such terrible arthritis that there were times I could hardly move. I was in pain all of the time, but the worst was in the winter, when the cold weather attacked my joints.

These visions took place in January. There were two of them, one day apart. Both of them happened the same way.

It was early in the morning when I woke up and saw two men standing at the foot of the bed. They had on white suits and they did not speak, but we could see them almost as though there was a light on them. I was scared to death, and when I reached over to awaken my husband, I could see that he was already awake and just as scared as I was. They stood there for a long time, maybe five minutes, and then they just disappeared.

This happened two nights in a row, and on both nights we had to get up and sit in a lighted room because we were so scared.

We didn't know what to make of it. About five days later I was awakened again, this time by a ball of light. This light came through the window and hovered above our bed. My husband watched it, too, and both of us were too frightened to run. It was there for a couple of minutes and then it just went away.

After the experience of light, Carol says, her arthritis went away and has never plagued her since. I found this experience astonishing. In talking to her husband and to people who know this woman, I have been able to confirm that her arthritis did indeed spontaneously disappear.

"IN THE NEAR LIGHT"

Sometimes the near-death experience itself can be shared with someone who is not near death. One of Germany's most noted poets, Karl Skala, had such an experience during World War II. He and his best friend were huddled together in a foxhole during an artillery bombardment.

The shells hit closer and closer until one finally hit close to Skala's friend and killed him. The poet felt his friend slump forward into his arms and go limp with death. Then a strange thing happened to Skala. He felt himself being drawn up with his friend, above their bodies and then above the battlefield.

Skala could look down and see himself holding his friend. Then he looked up and saw a bright light and felt himself going toward it with his friend. Then he stopped and returned to his body. He was uninjured except for hearing loss from the artillery blast.

After the war he wrote a poem about the incident, which I'll quote in full here. It is one of the most beautiful poems about a spiritual experience of this kind that I have ever read:

> *Would you really call this dying?*
> *In the near light, but far away.*
> *This light which our hope nurtures.*
> *To the star, high above*
> *everyone has traveled there in their mind*
> *before your body, the mind, the spirit*
> *belonged once to the stars*
> *let this light shine deep in your heart, in your dreams on*
> *this earth.*
> *Death is an awakening.*

SCIENCE, NOT POETRY

This is a lovely poem, but science is about hard facts, not poetry. As a clinician I know the worth of visions, especially deathbed visions. They empower the dying patient and his family and provide a meaning to the events that help heal the grief.

As a scientist I wanted to go beyond the clinical uses of

deathbed visions. I wanted to know if we could validate these visionary experiences using scientific methods. I began to jot down questions:

"Does precognition *really* occur?"

"Is it possible that pre-death visions have a basis in science?"

"Are psychic experiences real or made up after the fact?"

I jotted down these questions in a notebook, hoping to formulate a study someday that could answer them to my satisfaction. At this point I did not know that I was soon to become involved in a study that would answer them, one that was perhaps the most exciting of my career.

3

THE SIDS STUDY

Men fear death, as children fear to
go in the dark.

—Francis Bacon

A s a parent it is hard even to imagine the horror of having a child die of sudden infant death syndrome (SIDS). This condition is also known as crib death, because the child quite simply dies in his or her sleep. Death by SIDS is especially difficult for the surviving family members because it happens to seemingly healthy children. Often the child is put to bed and later found dead.

The cause of SIDS is a mystery. The most recent theory is that the child smothers in the bedsheets while lying on his stomach. Other theories include respiratory infection, metabolism problems, heartbeat disorder, a faulty brainstem, or overly sensitive airways in the lungs. These are all theories. The real cause of SIDS is unknown.

The loss of a child to SIDS is very distressing for the family. Parents feel guilty, thinking that they could somehow have prevented the death of their baby. Sometimes they blame each other, even though it is unclear why the child has died. Siblings often begin to fear that they, too, will die in their sleep. Their fear and sense of loss leads to nightmares, bad behavior, and feelings of guilt that they were somehow responsible for the death.

On top of all this parents often receive a visit from the coronor or the police department investigating the possibility of murder, especially when the death cannot be explained by autopsy.

The horror of SIDS has been studied from almost every angle. Medical science has examined its cause, while psychologists have looked at ways parents can cope with their grief. Yet nowhere in the reams of SIDS research I examined is there anything to do with premonitions of death, even as a factor in counseling. The absence of such material surprised me, because as a clinician I know that parents sometimes foresee the deaths of their children.

"SHE CAN'T KEEP THE BABY"

One such premonition comes from a woman I'll call Judy. She has two beautiful daughters who are my patients. When she was twenty-one years old, she and her husband were elated to find that she was pregnant. She marveled at the feeling of the baby growing inside her and couldn't wait to hold it in her arms.

When she was seven months pregnant, she had a puzzling vision, one that took place while she rested on her bed in the afternoon, fully awake. As she told it,

I suddenly found myself floating out of my body to the ceiling of the bedroom. I hovered in the air, looking down at myself. Suddenly I realized that there was a lady floating in the air next to me. She glowed with a soft white light.

The lady and I looked down at my body. It was as though that person on the bed was someone else. The lady began to talk about the person on the bed as though it wasn't me. "You know," she said with great love and compassion, "she can't keep the baby. It is going to die."

I wasn't angry. Instead I felt great love and compassion when she said that, as if this baby's death was part of a greater purpose and plan.

Less than a year later Judy's child died of SIDS.

VISIONARY OPPORTUNITY

Judy's story and others like it made me realize that SIDS parents might make an excellent group in which to study pre-death visions. In some ways the study of visions could also be considered a study of the unseen bonds between people. And what group has tighter bonds than parents and their children?

Still it would be hard to find the large number of SIDS parents necessary for the experimental group. Since SIDS happens in only three of every thousand babies born, it would be extremely time-consuming to find the dozens of parents necessary to conduct such a study. Still I didn't give up.

As the regional chairman of private-practice research for the American Academy of Pediatrics, I met with pediatricians all over the country to discuss ongoing research. At these meetings I mentioned the thought of enlisting SIDS parents into such a study. None of my colleagues was interested. Some thought it seemed "ghoulish," while others thought it "a waste of time."

I wasn't pleased by the response of my colleagues, but to an extent I could understand it. Medical research is based on taking one tiny step at a time. A study like this represented a giant leap, maybe into foolishness. After all, no one had even done anything close to looking for pre-death visions in parents whose children had died of SIDS. Such a study might look more like a leap of faith than a leap of science.

Finally I had a stroke of good fortune. In 1991 I met Carrie Sheehan, a dynamo of a woman who is associated with the Southwest SIDS Alliance. Carrie had had a child die of SIDS more than thirty years before and she has been working to combat this killer ever since.

The alliance is the country's largest research organization studying SIDS. They have conducted research into every possible cause of SIDS, including sleeping positions, medications, and prenatal factors.

Although she has never had any sort of vision associated with SIDS, she was interested in the paranormal. She asked me if I wanted to be involved in a study that would explore the possibility that SIDS parents have pre-death visions.

"Yes," I answered unequivocally.

I don't think she was expecting such a rapid affirmative response. She groped for words for a few moments and then said, "Is this easy for you to research? Don't other doctors think it's a little weird?"

She didn't realize I had been wanting to be involved in such a study for several years.

THE SIDS STUDY

As I thought about the SIDS study, I wondered if there were humanitarian values in researching such things as pre-death visions. Are there practical aspects to studying paranormal experiences, or were we just providing fodder for supermarket tabloids and TV talk shows?

I pondered these questions after accepting Carrie Sheehan's offer to help her study SIDS parents. I thought that we should take a look at these issues even if we looked foolish. I took solace in the words of scientist James Burke, who said that the "act of mystical significance, in which man discovers a fundamental fact about nature, is at the very heart of science." Perhaps this study would help to show that the paranormal isn't so "para" after all. And perhaps not. The only way to know would be to proceed.

The SIDS Alliance chose a brilliant method to get at this intimate question. They had designed a lengthy questionnaire to examine every possible factor contributing to SIDS death. Included were questions about drug and alcohol habits of the parents, sleeping positions of the children, dietary habits, genetic history, and so forth.

In the middle of this huge questionnaire was a single question: "Did you sense something was going to happen to your baby?" An astonishing 21 percent answered yes. A large number of those said that their premonitions were so strong or their visions so vivid that they wrote about them in their diaries. Some even told their physicians or ministers *before* the baby died.

"Big deal," you might say. "All parents have feelings of

dread about their infant children." I would have thought this also had we not administered a similar test to three control groups. Each of these groups consisted of parents with babies who did not die of SIDS or anything else. Only slightly more than 3 percent of these parents said that they had had premonitions that something harmful was going to happen to their child.

I found these results surprising. Almost one fifth of the parents who lost children to SIDS had had very strong premonitions of the death. That was 31 of the 174 families who responded to the study.

They decided to examine these premonitions further. Researchers in Texas gave an additional questionnaire to each of the parents in these thirty-one families and then followed up with a telephone interview.

A full report of this landmark study will be presented in a book by Richard Hardoin, M.D., and Judy Henslee, R.N., Ph.D., who were the principal investigators. The data has been presented at medical conferences.

The results that I can present offer a glimpse into the frequency and nature of this kind of experience:

■ *Seventeen of the respondents said that the premonition or "sensation" took place more than five times.* These premonitions amounted to dreams or feelings, or a combination of both.

■ *Twenty-two of the respondents said that the experience happened immediately before the death.* By "immediately before" we mean that the premonition happened within twenty-four hours before the death. For eight of these people the experience was so compelling that they visited their doctor or emergency room. Of these eight, four had a dream or vision that their baby died. Seven recorded the experience in a journal before the SIDS death. Remarkably, many of these parents told their experience to others before the death of their child.

- *Many of those in the study felt that they had witnessed a physical event.* Some felt that they had seen their child stop breathing for long periods of time while asleep.

- *Some were helped in grieving, some not, by the premonitions.* Although twenty-eight of the respondents said that the premonitions taught them to trust their own intuition, visions, or dreams, eighteen reported that the experience was negative for them. Rather than help them in their grief, the death-related visions created feelings of helplessness, fear, anger, and guilt. On the other hand nine of the respondents said that the premonitions had helped them grieve. This was especially true of those who had vivid dreams or visions. Said one mother whose child died of SIDS after such a premonition, "Even though I am grief-stricken, I feel a distant sense of comfort from my dream. It was almost as though it had happened before, for one thing; and almost as though it was meant to happen, for another."

The premonitions in the control group were far less vivid than those of the SIDS parents. For instance, one of the subjects had had two miscarriages and was of advanced maternal age. Her premonition amounted to a feeling that it would be just her luck if her baby died of SIDS. Some of those in the study group had family members who lost children to birth defects and feared the same fate for themselves. Others had lingering concerns about prenatal tests that indicated possible abnormalities. Only a few had a vivid dream that their baby would die, a dream that didn't come true.

VARIETIES OF EXPERIENCE

The interviews with the parents presented a more detailed picture of these premonitions. After examining each of these case studies, we were able to separate them into three categories: vague fears, vivid dreams, and outright visions.

In examining these I was impressed by the difference between the premonitions of the SIDS group and those of the control group. The visions and premonitions of most of the SIDS parents had a quality of hyperreality that made them unforgettable. As a SIDS mother told me, "The difference between my vision and a dream was like the difference between television and actually being there." This validates my previous study on the differences between true visions and premonitions that do not come true.

Category 1: Pervasive, Vague Fears

In this category of premonition there was no visionary experience or dream. Instead there was a nagging feeling that the baby was going to die or be "taken away."

Typical of experiences in this category was that of a twenty-nine-year-old woman who began to have feelings during her pregnancy that the child she was carrying would die of SIDS. These continued after the birth. For example, she was sitting on the couch playing and singing to her infant when she suddenly had an overwhelming feeling that her baby was going to die. This happened to her many times in the weeks previous to the child's death.

"I Had Thoughts That Seemed Crazy"

Another example of these vague yet pervasive fears of death comes from a thirty-nine-year-old physician with two living children. When his wife was pregnant with their third child, he became preoccupied with thoughts that the baby would die. "I had thoughts that seemed crazy," said the doctor.

On a regular basis he would drive by a cemetery on his way home from the office, even though it was far out of his way. The first time he held his newborn son, he had the distinct impression that "this baby was not supposed to have been born."

A few days before the baby died, the mother and child took a trip across the country. When the father held his child and kissed him good-bye, he heard a voice that said, "Look at him, you will not see him again." He gave the baby to his wife and again heard the voice say, "Stop, don't let him go."

The night the baby died, the father awoke thinking about SIDS.

"That morning, when my wife called me, she was screaming and delirious," said the doctor. "But I was not surprised, since I had felt it all along."

Although I would be inclined to categorize this as a visionary experience from my own perspective, the doctor did not feel that this was a vision. Rather he insisted that it was a "feeling or intuition without cause." He said that the voice he heard was his own.

"I have never had a similar experience and I have no idea of the meaning of this one," he said. "The only thing that I can say is that perhaps I should have listened to my heart."

He called these persistent visions "vague" fears, although they seemed quite specific. The control study groups show that such an experience is not common at all, but actually quite rare.

"I Am Not Going to Keep You"

A number of women reported frequent sensations that their child would die before it actually did. For instance a thirty-two-year-old woman with two children kept sensing that her child was going to die. On one occasion she was sitting on the bed with her baby when she suddenly said out loud, "I am not going to get to keep you, am I?" She had no idea why she said that. Another time she was driving her car when she was overwhelmed with feelings that her daughter would die.

Others became so obsessed with their feelings that something was wrong that they made frequent visits to doctors. Even though the doctors found nothing wrong with their children, these women insisted that something was wrong. The result was a lot of anger toward their physicians. "I became very mad at my doctor," said one of the women. "He listens to me now and even says that the death of my child made him believe that a mother has a special bond with her child, but when it counted, he wouldn't listen to me."

CATEGORY 2: VIVID DREAMS

In this category the death of the child is seen in a dream. Typically this dream is extremely realistic, so much so that the person who has it cannot dismiss the experience.

Sometimes the person may not be sleeping when this dream takes place. He or she may be dozing on the bed or sitting alone in a quiet room in a half-awake state called hypnagogia, a highly creative state of mind between sleeping and wakefulness.

Many people are thought to be in a state of hypnagogia when they have paranormal experiences. In my own research I have encountered many cases in which a person has a visionary encounter in the hypnagogic state. It came as no surprise to me that so many of these premonitions took place at the point of going to sleep.

"The Murderer Came Twice"

A thirty-five-year-old woman had such dreams. Her child was five months old when she had identical dreams about him being killed by an unseen intruder. The first dream took place about two weeks before the child died, the second only the night before. Here is how she described it:

In my dream I awoke from my sleep and could hear someone breaking in the front door. I knew what was going on, especially since they made so much noise, but I couldn't move. I just lay there, paralyzed, and listened as this person came into the house. I could hear him walking slowly down the hall to my baby's room and then a few minutes later I heard him run down the hall and back out the door. I knew what he had done, he had killed my baby. There was nothing I could do. I started crying and then I woke up. This dream happened two times, so the murderer came twice.

This was an extremely vivid dream for this woman. She told her husband and some of her friends about her dream and even confessed that it seemed to foretell events. Now this woman feels as though she should have acted on the dream even though she is not sure how. "I knew the dream meant something, I just wasn't sure what," she said. "The dream made me afraid, but it didn't tell me what to be afraid of."

"I Saw Where She Was Going"

A woman I'll call Linda told of having a vision of "heaven" at the same instant her infant daughter died of SIDS. This experience happened almost fifty years ago, before SIDS was really acknowledged. Linda had a tremendous amount of guilt over the death of her child, as do many parents whose children die of this syndrome. Yet her grief was greatly relieved by a "sort of vision or dream" that she had at the same moment her daughter died. Here is her story:

I was in my early twenties when Kathy died. I had no reason to expect that anything was wrong. I fed her and burped her like I always did and then put her down to sleep in the crib.

I went to bed myself about an hour later. I was tired like most new mothers are and I went right to sleep. All of a sudden it was like I was there. I could see a beautiful country that seemed to be made of light. The hills and grass and sky were spectacular. There were various shades of light that glowed in the most generous way.

I could see my daughter there in this field, a place that looked like a meadow. She wasn't lying there, but she wasn't walking either. Maybe she was floating.

I felt as though I had finally come home, as though this "beyond" place was where I should be. And then I woke up.

Linda awoke with a start. She knew that this dream meant something and was afraid that it meant her child was in danger. She tumbled from her bed and ran to Kathy's crib, where she found the baby dead.

Needless to say, the child's death was extremely traumatizing. Linda and her husband sold the house as quickly as they could and she has never driven past it again. Still, there was a comforting aspect to this vision that Linda did not ignore.

"When things got tough, I thought of that dream," said Linda. "It helped me overcome the pain because I know that I saw where she was going."

"You Will Live Through It"

Other women reported "warning" dreams in which they saw their children being killed by strangers or even family members. One reported a dream in which her mother had "sucked up" her son into a vacuum cleaner. As the child's mother held the dead baby in the bag, her mother said, "I know this is hard, but you will live through it."

The next morning she told her husband of the dream and said it made her "sick to her soul." She felt that it was a premonition of some kind, but went to work anyway. Her baby-sitter called her later that afternoon to tell her that the baby had died.

A number of the vivid dreams involved seeing the child in a casket hours before the child actually died.

These dreams have a vividness to them that led one woman to say, "If your dreams are so real that you can't get them out of your mind, then pay attention to them. It would have helped me keep my little boy alive."

CATEGORY 3: SPIRITUAL VISIONS

This form of vision involves elements described as being strongly spiritual by the people having them. Most often they describe a vivid dream accompanied by a voice. Sometimes they sense a being of light or a deceased family member standing with them as they admire their child. The spiritual elements in these cases are the voice and the presence of the being of light or the deceased family member.

The presence of a voice or being of light are not the only elements that define these premonitions as spiritual. Sometimes the person having these death-related visions will refer to them as spiritual experiences just because he or she feels that way. I realize that this is a subjective measure of spirituality, but I don't think there is any other way to measure it, since spirituality is in the eye of the beholder.

I encountered one such experience at a talk I gave in the Midwest. I'll call this woman Nan.

Nan is a forty-five-year-old married woman with two children. When she was thirty-eight, her newborn son died of SIDS. Although she was extremely distraught by her child's death and stated often during our conversation that she would never get over it, she said that it was not unexpected. While sitting quietly in her living room only a week before the baby died, she had a vision of what was going to take place:

I was sitting in my living room reading a paperback book. The baby was asleep in his crib, and I was resting because I had been up half the night with his fussiness. As I was sitting there in the quiet, I had the feeling that I was not alone. I wasn't afraid, I just wasn't alone.

I looked up and there was my father. He had been dead for a year, but there he stood. For some reason I wasn't surprised at all. He was just there for a second or two, but I heard him tell me, "Jason is coming with me." I knew exactly what he meant. He meant that my baby was going to die.

Nan told her husband and her best friend what had happened. She insisted that it was a premonition and that her baby would soon die.

"I felt some guilt about my child's death," she told me. "I

really believed the vision, but then I didn't believe it, do you know what I mean? I just couldn't quite put my faith in it."

"I Saw the Casket and the Tombstone"

Another example of a spiritual vision comes from a woman who attended one of my talks in California. From almost the moment she had her fourth child, this woman, whom I'll call Terry, felt that this child would die. "Something didn't seem right," she said. "I couldn't tell you what it was, but I had a feeling that I wouldn't get to keep this baby."

About two nights before the baby died, Terry had a dream that directly foretold this child's death:

> In this dream I could see that I was walking across a field of grass. I kept walking and walking until I came right upon a little casket. "Who is this?" I thought. Then I looked ahead a little farther and I could see my son's gravestone.

The dream was incredibly vivid, but Terry still interpreted it as a dream. "Now I wish I had acted on it somehow, but how? What could I really have done?"

Feelings of helplessness about these visions are common ones. A woman in the study reported seeing her child's name on a tombstone while she was awake, but didn't know what to do about it. Another woman had a waking vision that "someone" came to her bedside and told her that there would be a death in the family. She recorded this vision in a journal, but thought it was referring to her father.

Despite the feelings of helplessness that these visions frequently convey, those who have them often say that they are comforted by their "spiritual nature," the general sense that there is a meaning to life and death that we only get hints of through events such as death-related visions.

"SO WHAT?"

Skepticism abounds around studies like this one. I told a colleague about it, and he just snorted. "So what?" he said. "Don't you think that these 'premonitions' are just wishful thinking? Don't you think that they were just looking for something spiritual to come out of their kid's death? Doesn't every parent have a fear or premonition that their child will die of SIDS?"

"Maybe in some cases," I said. "But how do you explain that many of these people told others of their experience before the child's death?"

"I don't know," he said with a shrug.

"And how about the seven who wrote down the experience in a journal *before* the death? How do you explain that?"

"I don't know," he said.

"And how about the eight people who visited the emergency room or their doctor because of their visions? And how do you explain that twenty-two of them reported their fears to someone else less than twenty-four hours before the death?"

"Okay, maybe there is some truth to this," said my fellow physician. "But what am I supposed to do with this information?"

Good question, I thought. Considering the large number of people who openly and curiously talk about death-related visions, maybe the main message of the study is a simple one: *Listen patiently to the people who have these experiences.* They, too, are puzzled by what has happened. Together you might be able to give meaning to the events.

4

THE CIRCUIT BOARDS
OF MYSTICISM
REVISITED

The brain has not explained the mind fully.

—Wilder Penfield, M.D.

A nurse from a community hospital in the Northwest came to me with a puzzling experience.

She had a ten-year-old patient who had been burned over 80 percent of his body in a house fire. He had spent several weeks at the burn center of a major hospital and had become stable enough to be transferred to this smaller hospital, which was closer to his home. After a few days there he died suddenly of an infection that his weakened immune system could not fight off.

No one had expected this boy to die. Indeed he had been moved to this hospital because his condition had improved so greatly.

Actually I shouldn't say that no one had expected it—the nurse who spoke to me did. For two nights before he passed away, this nurse saw a woman in white standing at the burned boy's bedside.

The first night she saw the lady in white, the nurse thought she was an unauthorized visitor. As the nurse approached, the woman disappeared.

The next night she saw the woman again. This time she was standing at the foot of the boy's bed talking to him. The nurse watched for a few seconds and then approached the room. Again the woman disappeared.

The next night the boy became very sick and died. The doctors were in a panic as he began to fade away. They had spent the day trying to stop the infection that was ravaging their patient. Now, as he lay dying, they spent ninety minutes trying to revive him.

While the doctors, nurses, and respiratory therapists struggled to bring the boy back, an abrasive physician found fault with everyone's work. As they stood around the boy's dead body, this distressed physician gave everyone the impression that it was their fault that the boy had died.

Events combined to make this stressful day one of the worst of this nurse's life. Everyone left the room and went their separate ways. She went into a utility room to cry. About half an hour later she came out of the room and headed for the nurses' station. There ahead of her she saw the little boy, walking hand-in-hand with the woman in white.

JUST WHAT HAD HAPPENED?

The nurse did not know what to make of these sightings. Such a thing had never happened to her before, nor has it happened since. "Most of the time I chalk this vision off to exhaustion," she told me. "Then sometimes I think that the woman was a visual metaphor, that there were signs that the boy was gravely ill and only my unconscious mind recognized them, and that it created the woman in white. Then sometimes I think it was a spiritual being who came to make death easier on the boy. I just don't know."

Just what was it that happened to this nurse? Had her mind created a guardian angel for the boy, or had she been able to see an actual angel?

Questions like this one peck at the very core of research into visionary experience. Anyone who examines death-related visions comes away with the same question: Does the human brain create visionary experiences, or does it receive them telepathically in an area of the brain where the material and spiritual worlds meet?

This is a sticky question, because it can be fairly answered either way. After examining thousands of case studies, and even after having had a death-related vision of my own, I can say without a doubt that the brain *both* creates visionary experiences *and* detects them. There seems to be a huge area of the brain that is devoted to having just such experiences. Just as we have a region of our brain devoted to speech and one that helps us regain our balance when we trip and almost fall, we have an area that is devoted to communication with the mystical. It functions as a sort of sixth sense. In short, it is the "God sensor."

MY OWN STORY:
A VISION OF MY FATHER

I have had a visionary experience of my own, so I have seen firsthand the mysterious ways in which this area of the brain works.

In 1988 my father appeared to me when he died. The first knowledge I had of his death was through this vision.

Here is what happened:

One night in January I came home late from the hospital. It had been a very difficult day and I was only interested in sleep. I turned off my beeper and my telephone and told my wife that I didn't want to be disturbed for any reason. Then I went to bed.

As I fell asleep in the darkened room, my father appeared to me in a dream. He just stood there facing me. He spoke very clearly. "Melvin, call your answering service. I have something to tell you."

I awoke with a start and charged into the living room. "My dad just told me to call my answering service," I said to my wife. I made the call and was told that my mother had been trying to reach me with an urgent message. It was to tell me that my father had died.

Since that very personal event I have had little doubt that the human brain has the ability to communicate telepathically. It is *how* these paranormal events take place that baffles me.

A FROG'S EYE
VIEW OF REALITY

Maybe paranormal events such as telepathy and visions can be understood if we think of them as an opening up of our ability to comprehend reality. By that I mean that there is much more happening around us than our brains can perceive.

A study done by MIT scientists demonstrates what I am talking about. The brains of frogs were wired with sensitive electronic equipment to allow researchers to perceive how frogs actually take in the world. The view was quite different from the one you and I share as we look at the world around us.

Frogs don't see beautiful forests or desert vistas. They perceive the things necessary to their survival, such as shadows that could mark the arrival of a predator, or the sound and sight of something buzzing around that might be edible. Their reality is greatly "screened down" from ours.

It is not hard to imagine that our reality is greatly screened down as well. Philosophers and scientists agree that we perceive only a small amount of the sensory data that occur around us all the time. As the neurophysiologist Sir John Eccles stated so eloquently, "By far, the greater part of the activity in the brain . . . does not reach consciousness at all."

Aldous Huxley compared the way we filter input to a reducing valve, one that leaves only a "measly trickle" of information by which to form our reality. He admitted that this trickle provides "at least [a] sufficient picture of reality." He also believed that this valve could be opened with "spiritual exercises" and "innate gift," which I interpret to mean such things as death-related visions.

Since philosophers and scientists agree that there are more sensory data than we normally perceive, you would think that the study of the paranormal would be respectable. After all, there are many things to explore scientifically in this field. Maybe it is just our obsession with reliability that makes the study of the paranormal seem like a futile activity. As Eccles wrote, "I think telepathy is still a tenable belief [but] . . . it provides an extremely imperfect and inefficient way of transferring information from the neural activity of [the brain]."

For too many of us this area of the brain—the circuit boards of mysticism, as I call them—has fallen into disuse. In an odd way we are similar to primitive human beings, who have the ability to comprehend subjects such as math but have just never been exposed to mathematical concepts. Few modern people have developed these circuit boards of mysticism.

SHARED VISIONS OF DEATH

Shared visions offer some of the best examples of the power to communicate that is contained in this portion of the brain. In the type of shared visions I am talking about, one person's death experience is shared by another. The other person doesn't physically die, but somehow the consciousness of the dying person is shared through clairvoyance.

I will discuss a number of such visions here. The first comes from an article in the journal *Nursing '92*.

The article was written by Linda Houlberg, a nurse in Oak Ridge, Tennessee, who tells of a close relationship she had had with a patient named Virginia.

Virginia was dying of cancer, fighting against the pain because her husband and two sons wanted her to keep on living.

But the pain had become too much for her; now she just wanted to die.

"I'm ready," she told her good friend, Houlberg.

Houlberg had spent a lot of time with Virginia. She was a hospice nurse and had hit it off immediately with this patient. Over their months together she had watched her deteriorate, losing weight and strength to her disease. As her illness progressed, Virginia lost her fear of death and began to accept it.

Virginia worked out many of her feelings about dying through her painting. One of those paintings was entitled *The Light at the End of the Tunnel.* It was a tunnel of light that represented what she thought would happen to her when she died.

On the night Virginia died, Houlberg went to bed at about twelve-thirty. At twelve fifty-five she awoke and looked at the clock. At that moment she thought that Virginia was dead. Then, as she writes,

> All of a sudden I saw her painting as clear as day. I felt her presence beside me, and I could see the tunnel in my mind's eye. We began moving down the tunnel together, passing by the blue-and-black sides of the painting. I could see the yellow light at the end of the tunnel, and as we got closer, the light became brighter and whiter.

They reached the end of the tunnel together and broke into a field of bright light. Then Houlberg realized that she couldn't stay with her friend. "It isn't my time," she wrote. "I still have things to do."

In the morning Virginia's son called to tell Houlberg that his mother had died at one A.M.

Houlberg sums up her own experience nicely:

I can't explain what happened to me. My psychic side says that I had an out-of-body experience, that Virginia was afraid to go through the tunnel alone, so she recruited me to accompany her. My logical side says that's foolish. But it doesn't really matter. What matters is that I knew without any doubt that Virginia was with God—and feeling great.

"I WILL BE TAKING JEANNIE WITH ME"

Another shared death experience comes from the work of Dr. Earnest Hyslop, a professor of ethics and logic at Columbia University at the turn of the century. Hyslop was one of the founders of the American Society of Psychical Research, the prestigious scientific organization devoted to research into the paranormal.

One of the cases he investigated was that of two girls who were dying of diphtheria in June 1889. The first girl, Jeannie, died several hours before her friend. The second girl, Edith, was not told of the death of Jeannie.

As Edith was on her deathbed, she had a vision of her friend. While in the visionary state the two had a conversation, and Edith knew that Jeannie had passed before her.

"Father, you did not tell me that Jeannie was already there," she said to her surprised father, who was at her bedside. He said that she stretched her arms out and smiled. "I will be taking Jeannie with me."

Hyslop documented over one hundred such cases, personally interviewing people present at the death and documenting the specifics of various cases. I have documented many such cases in my own files.

This book is filled with stories from my own files that fit into this category. I will offer two more here to illustrate exactly what I mean.

"I Know, I Know"

A twenty-four-year-old woman I'll call Jill was having an extremely traumatic labor. The doctors gave her a spinal anesthetic when they decided to deliver the baby by cesarean section. The anesthetic unexpectedly spread up her back, effectively paralyzing her entire body. The anesthesiologist acted quickly, so she was never deprived of oxygen and was never considered clinically near death. She was given no drugs that might have caused hallucinations.

However, during the delivery she felt drawn out of her body and into a glowing ball of light. While she was in that light, a voice "filled with love" spoke loudly to her. "You have to go back," the voice said. "But I am keeping the baby here with me. She will be safe here."

When the doctors told her that her baby girl was stillborn and had never taken her first breath of life, she told them that she already knew and explained what had happened. She told her doctors that she had been in a ball of light with her child and that she knew God would be taking care of her.

"Through the Bedroom Wall"

Another such case is that of a man I'll call Paul. At the age of twenty-one he was nearly beaten to death with a tire iron. The beating left him with more than a dozen skull fractures and two badly fractured arms.

He was left for dead late at night and isn't sure exactly how long he was unconscious. When he awoke, he found himself in the company of a man he calls a guardian angel. The man helped him get to a farmhouse that was about a mile away and then he disappeared.

Paul was taken to the hospital, where he was given little chance of surviving. During the next six hours he experienced four cardiac arrests and was told by doctors that he would never be normal again. Still Paul recovered, and within a year he was living a fairly normal life.

One aspect of his life that was not normal, however, was the visions he had. It was not uncommon for him to lapse into a visionary state and see things before they happened.

The most interesting of these was the one that took place at the home of his future in-laws. He was sitting alone in the living room when he suddenly went into a dreamlike state in which he saw an accident involving a car. The vision was not entirely clear, but it looked like a car covered with bricks and other debris.

When he came out of his trance, his girlfriend and her parents were standing at the entrance to the room, just staring at him. The father said that the room was so cold, they had been unable to come in.

Paul told his in-laws about his vision. Since they were leaving on vacation the next day, they took it as a sign that they should not leave until at least another day had passed.

The next night, as they lay sleeping in their bed, a drunk driver came down the street and lost control of his car. The car drove through the brick wall of the house and stopped at the foot of the surprised parents' bed.

I don't think it requires a leap of faith at all to acknowledge the obvious significance of such experiences. What we realize through experiences such as these is the truth of Meister Eckhart's dictum, "God is at the center of Man."

LINK WITH THE DIVINE

Most scientists and physicians do not agree with me on this point. Skeptics believe that experiences such as the ones described above are the result of abnormal brain activity. Dr. Arnold Mandell, a neurobiologist, believes that a human brain under stress releases neurotransmitters that trip a safety mechanism that makes it possible to deal with stress and trauma. Although stating that the Kingdom of God can be found in our right temporal lobe, his writings imply that no corresponding God exists outside our right temporal lobe.

I agree with Mandell's assertion that these neurotransmitters are released by the brain under stress, but I don't think it stops there. I think the evidence is clear that this area of our brain allows us to access another, even larger reality. When this area of the brain is stimulated, it triggers normal brain processes that happen to be visionary.

THE INDEPENDENT HALVES OF THE BRAIN

In essence humans have two separate brains. Most modern neurobiologists accept the concept that there are two separate brains. Their work shows that our left temporal lobes and deep related structures are concerned with language and communication. William Calvin, the noted neurobiologist, feels that this side of the brain makes up thoughts that we think to ourselves, our internal narrator. The other half of our brain is responsible for nonverbal thought, such as spatial concepts.

These two brains work fairly independently of each other. Sometimes, when the two halves are separated, it is difficult to tell that the person is operating on only half a brain.

As a medical student at Johns Hopkins University I studied a case in which a young boy had had half his brain removed as a treatment for seizures. He seemed so normal after his surgery that only sophisticated neurological tests could detect any difference in his functioning.

Numerous studies on people with surgically split brains have shown that the two halves of the brain act somewhat independently and somewhat cooperatively. For example a centerfold from *Playboy* magazine was shown to a man after a split-brain operation to cure his intractable epilepsy. The centerfold was shown only to the nonverbal right side of the brain by covering the man's right eye (which sends information to the left side of the brain). When the man was asked what he saw, the verbal left brain answered by saying, "I don't know what I'm seeing, but I know it's great. Show it to me again."

It is difficult to explain these sorts of clinical findings without speculating that a unitary consciousness overrides the entire nervous system. This is something that a neurobiologist might call an integrating neuroelectric force field or that a philosopher might call a soul.

I have long felt that if the human soul resides anywhere, it is in the right temporal lobe. It is this area of the brain that produced out-of-body experiences when probed during surgery. Neurosurgeon Wilder Penfield, one of the first to map the brain, stimulated this area and found that patients actually declared that they were "half in and half out" of their bodies.

Penfield's research also linked this area of the brain with psychic experiences.

His mentor, Hughlings Jackson, called the temporal lobe the source of "psychical seizures." Stimulation in this area of the brain unleashed "dreamy states," such as déjà vu and mystical consciousness.

I also think it is this area of the brain that allows many people to escape the horrors that life can deal up. In some ways these could be described as an escape hatch for our consciousness.

The temporal lobe's function is often death related, but not always. Having a vision that heals cancer is one such example of the type of experience that might spring from this region of the brain. Precognitive experiences happen, too, such as seeing a bus crash before it takes place. Some people have even been consoled during physical trauma by their visions. Also seen are those who claim that an actual guardian angel prevented them from being harmed.

All of these are events that I believe spring from our "circuit board of mysticism."

"I Was Beside Myself with Fear"

Such an event was told to me by the wife of a nationally known talk-show host, who spoke to me after I appeared on her husband's show. With a nervous smile on her face she told me how a guardian angel had rescued her from certain rape:

My car broke down at night on a busy freeway, and I had to pull far off the road. I sat and waited for a while until a car pulled in front of me. I wanted to wait for the police, so I just waved to him through the window to go on. He kept coming back, and I thought that maybe he just didn't see me, so I rolled the window down to tell him that I wanted to wait for the police. When I did that, he reached into the car and took my keys.

When I protested, he slapped me and told me to move over, then he got in and pulled out a gun. He put the gun against my side and told me to take off my pantyhose and underwear.

I was beside myself with fear. I didn't want to be raped and I didn't want to be shot, but I was afraid that both of them were going to happen no matter what I did. I tried to do what he wanted me to do, but I was starting to break down emotionally and he was getting mad.

All of a sudden the car filled with this bright, bright light. I thought a car had pulled up behind us, but I looked back and saw nothing. Then the rapist said, "Oh my God!" and when he said that, I realized that the light was coming from inside the car, right there between us. A man appeared in the light. I was glad to see him. It was like I had always known him and felt comfortable with him. But when that happened, the rapist opened the door and ran. He got in his car and left. When that happened, the light and the man disappeared, and I was left alone in the dark.

"WEIRD EVENTS," SUBJECTIVE REALITY

As you can see by now, reality can be extremely subjective. If we were there watching the events in that car, would we have seen the light or the man that appeared? Could we have taken a picture of him? Probably not. Yet I have no doubt from the woman's story that both she and her attacker saw the light and the guardian angel in it. Just as two people can share a near-death experience, I believe that her attacker shared this trauma-induced vision and fled the scene because of it.

What happened in this story was indeed paranormal, but in no way do I think it was fantasy. I simply think that we have a part of our brain that is in touch with what some consider to be mystical things. This area turns on at times of death and sometimes at times of danger. It also transmits knowledge. Dr. Jonas Salk, one of the inventors of the polio vaccine, calls this area of the brain our connection to "cosmic consciousness." He thinks that highly evolved people are able to tap into this area at certain times. For him these times are usually when he awakes late at night and begins writing down messages that he feels come from another realm. Over the years Salk has collected more than twelve thousand pages of these communications. Much of the knowledge he used to develop the polio vaccine came from information gleaned while in these altered states.

Others have found valuable knowledge while in the same sort of altered state. During a dream Albert Einstein saw himself riding a beam of light. He concluded after awakening that light would remain static if he were to do so, a theory that was against all the laws of physics at the time. This became the basis of his theory of relativity.

An altered state of consciousness was responsible for the invention of the benzene ring by Kekule von Stradonitz. While dozing in front of a fire he suddenly envisioned atoms forming snakes that then turned and bit their own tails. That led to his understanding of the chemical structure of benzene, which led to the development of the textile industry in Germany.

At an international convention of organic chemists Kekule

encouraged his fellow chemists to "dream, to dream, and to listen to our dreams."

Dr. Raymond Moody, the father of near-death studies, has developed techniques to tap into these circuit boards of mysticism. His technique is too involved to go into in detail, but it has proven to be a very effective way of inducing visions through meditation.

Many of the visions induced by Moody can be thought of as products of the mind. But others certainly seem to connect the patient with a mystical consciousness outside the body.

In one of his better-known case studies Moody induced a vision in television talk-show host Joan Rivers. Toward the end of her visionary encounter with a number of people in her life, Rivers had an out-of-body experience and reported that she traveled across the country to Los Angeles, where she found herself in the living room of her daughter's home. She said that she could hear her daughter taking a shower.

She immediately telephoned her daughter and let the telephone ring a number of times. Just as she was about to hang up, her daughter answered and said that she had been in the shower.

Moody has reported a number of cases like this one. His Theater of the Mind, in Alabama, is one good example of research facilities devoted to understanding this intriguing area of the brain that Salk calls "the source of my guidance."

This portion of the brain has also been pressed into service by researchers looking for new ways of dealing with problems such as depression. The methods they have used to stimulate it are unique and the results of their research are amazing. As I have found in my own research, these people truly were transformed by the light.

THE RIGHT-BRAIN CLINICAL PRACTICE

These transformations occurred during a series of bold experiments done after World War II that have been all but forgotten by the medical establishment. Yet they prove to me the healing power of these right-brained visions.

They were carried out by Dr. Joseph Atkinson, a specialist in gastroenterology, who was a member of the faculty of Northwestern University in Illinois. His specialty was the study of peptic ulcers. He felt that the established method of treating this disease was incomplete because it really only dealt with the symptom, which was the ulcer itself. Many people with ulcers, he said, had diseases of personality that made them angry, depressed, and unhappy. Get rid of their personality problems and you will get rid of their ulcers, he declared.

With a professor of pharmacology to help him, Atkinson created a mixture of gases that consisted of carbon dioxide and oxygen. They called it the Meduna mixture, after L. J. Meduna, a Hungarian physician who first developed it for use in treating such problems as stuttering.

Treatment was simple. It consisted of several sessions, in which patients breathed the gas for only a few seconds each. These patients frequently sensed that they were dying and reported moving up a tunnel and seeing a bright light, much like a near-death experience. In all the years that it was used, no patients died during treatment. Typical of the carbon-dioxide-therapy experiences is this case study from Meduna's research:

> I had an impression of being in complete understanding and harmony with God. Seemed like an abrupt awakening of truths I should have known but somehow hadn't known before. Fail-

ures and successes faded into insignificance and I was part of an all-consuming Love—so strong and intense and beautiful—everything was right—always had been right—only human's thoughts, errors and miscomprehensions of the Plan distorted facts and made the misery and unhappiness that is part of our lives. When I woke, I couldn't describe my sensations; while asleep, however, I still felt the effects and also a beautiful calm peace which lasted for several hours.

Psychosomatic complaints virtually disappeared with carbon-dioxide therapy, and the patients underwent personality transformations that were remarkably similar to those in people who have had near-death experiences. Most important was that their ulcers frequently healed.

So successful was the mixture that Atkinson and his colleagues thought it should be made available as an inexpensive alternative to conventional psychotherapy. A few sessions of the Meduna mixture often produced better results than dozens of hours of therapy.

It was used for twenty years and then dropped as a form of therapy when Atkinson retired. The Meduna mixture never caught on with other doctors. Not only did they not understand how it worked, but psychiatrists were not fond of a medical treatment that cut down on the need for a talking cure.

I have reviewed the Meduna mixture with Dr. Don Tyler, professor of anesthesiology at Seattle Children's Hospital, who feels that breathing the mixture for a few minutes could result in death. Based on my assessment, I believe that the Meduna mixture induced a near-death state that activated the right temporal lobe. The result was that these people were transformed by death-related visions.

THE CORE OF OUR SPIRIT

Through my examination of visionary experiences and death-related visions I have concluded that they are all born of the same neuronal machinery. Common threads run through them all: near-death experiences, shared near-death experiences, healing visions, postdeath visitations, and visions that warn of impending death. I have come to believe that they are all cut from the same cloth. This conclusion was reached after extensive research.

In one study at Seattle Children's Hospital I compared a number of children who had almost died with children who were seriously ill. I wanted to know if those who were seriously ill reported the classic elements of the near-death experience. In my study the children who were seriously ill reported none of the experiences of those patients who almost died.

This study proved that near-death experiences are not simply caused by a lack of oxygen to the brain, since many of those who were seriously ill in the study had also had low levels of oxygen in their blood. Furthermore it showed that near-death experiences are not related to drugs, the perception of dying, sensory deprivation, or psychological stress—all things that some scientists have assumed cause near-death experiences.

This study indicated that the so-called near-death experience is indeed the dying experience. It proved that it is not just the desperate antics of a brain low on oxygen. Near-death experiences also appeared to be transformative, deeply changing the people who have had them. As one patient in the study told me, "No matter how bad my life gets, I'll always know I have a friend in that light."

As I heard more and more of these stories, I decided to study the nature of the transformation in those who had had near-death experiences. I developed a three-hour battery of psychological tests designed to determine whether a person has truly had a near-death experience and how much of a transformation in personality actually occurred. These tests were administered to several hundred adults who had had near-death experiences as children. I wanted to see what happened to these children when they grew up and became adults.

As a means of comparison I also gave the tests to people who had been seriously ill, yet not near death, as well as several groups who had experienced other paranormal events, including a variety of visions, lucid dreams, and spontaneous healings. Over all, more than five hundred people have taken the battery of tests.

The results were significant. People who have near-death experiences are transformed in a number of ways. Their fear of death is half that of the normal population, and they have a zest for living that is so high that many consider themselves "life-aholics." Significantly, near-death experiencers have four times the number of *verifiable* psychic experiences of the normal population. A verifiable psychic experience is one that can be validated by other people.

They are transformed in other measurable ways as well. They give more money to charity, take fewer over-the-counter medications, exercise and meditate more, and eat more vegetables than the control groups.

This battery of tests allowed me to do a number of things. I could distinguish between a person who truly was dying and one who had had a "fear death" experience, a psychological response to the thought of dying. These tests enabled me to compare a wide range of visionary experiences to the near-death experience. I found to my great surprise that many such experiences proved to be as transformative as the near-death experience.

For example, those who had any sort of visionary experience of a loving light tested virtually the same as those who had had near-death experiences. This was an exciting find for me, that near-death experiences do not simply give us insight into what it is like to die; they are also the cornerstone of understanding visions. Pre-death visions, post-death visions, shared-death experiences, and the host of other mystical experiences are all related.

It doesn't seem to matter whether a person has a vision as he is dying or while he is near someone else who is dying; while he is sleeping or when he is in a state of spiritual crisis—the same sort of visions take place, with the same effects on the person having them.

TRUTH, NOT MYTH

I could now see that in all of the visions I have encountered during my studies, the same images of light and of the beings that dwell within it appear again and again, and the same insights and knowledge result. This has happened down through history.

Perhaps most notable is the vision of heaven that Saint Paul the Apostle wrote about in the Bible:

> I know a man in Christ who fourteen years ago was caught up into the third heaven—whether in the body or out of the

body I do not know, God knows. And I know that this man was caught up into Paradise—whether in the body or out of the body I do not know. God knows—and he heard things that cannot be told, which man may not utter. (2 Corinthians, 12:1–4)

Paul was privileged to have this glimpse of heaven without having to be near death. Yet the vision of heaven that he had resembles those of people who are lying on their deathbed. For example the often-quoted Mormon *Journal of Discourses* records the dying experience of Jedediah Grant, a church leader, as told to Heber Kimball:

> He said to me, Brother Heber, I have been into the spirit world two nights in succession, and of all the dreads that ever came across me, the worst was to have to return to my body, though I had to do it.
> He [Grant] saw his wife, she was the first person that came to him. He saw many that he knew, but did not have conversation with any but his wife, Caroline. She came to him and he said that she looked beautiful and had their little child, that died on the plains, in her arms, and said, "Mr. Grant, here is little Margaret; you know that the wolves ate her up; but it did not hurt her, here she is all right."

I was excited by this insight, although I realized that it was nothing new. After all, visions have been recounted for thousands of years. These visions have created institutions such as religions that have shaped societies; they have guided world leaders and even helped rulers lead great armies, as in the case of Joan of Arc.

Indeed visions have even defeated great armies. Among the

most memorable of these visions is the well-documented Angels of Mons, who appeared on a battlefield to troops in World War I. The Allies were in the midst of a terrible defeat with heavy casualties. Wounded soldiers were being taken to a hospital, where one after the other they told the puzzled nurses that they had seen angels on the battlefield. British soldiers said that the angel was Saint George and described him as having yellow hair and golden armor and riding on a white horse. French soldiers claimed they saw the Archangel Michael riding a white horse.

After the war the Germans offered their side of the story. Cavalry troops said that their horses suddenly refused to pursue the enemy and instead "turned sharply and fled." They also claimed that the Allied position they were attacking was held by thousands of troops, when in fact there were only two regiments present.

REAL AND TRANSFORMATIVE

Research such as the SIDS study offers statistical proof that precognitive visions do take place. My own research proves not only that death-related visions are real but that they transform the people who have them and often even leave them with the ability to sense other events before they happen.

In addition this research convinces me that there is a place in the human brain where the worlds of the physical and mystical come together. We have everything to gain and little to lose by opening ourselves up to mystical experiences.

For example, an emergency room nurse told me about a young man who was brought to the hospital with a gunshot wound. Although the wound did not appear to be life-threatening, the young man could not be consoled. He kept crying and asking this nurse to hold his hand. "I am going to die," he insisted.

She told him that was nonsense. "Don't be silly," she said. "This wound is nothing. You'll be okay."

"No, no, you don't understand," he said. "I won't be here when you get back."

About an hour later he died on the way to the X-ray department.

Visions are often described as being a "relief" or an explanation for something. Many people say these experiences are suddenly like "seeing the world as a whole" or like "perceiving things that are already there." The word *surreal* doesn't describe these visionary experiences so much as does *hyperreal*. As one man described it, "I felt like I was reaching out and touching all of reality."

In many ways science and philosophy agree with this definition of the paranormal. I have come across many studies in different fields that lend credence to the belief that there is more going on than meets the eye—or the other four senses, for that matter.

A HEALING FORCE

For example studies have shown that heart attack patients recover faster and go home from the hospital sooner if people pray for them, even strangers. Exactly why this happens isn't known, but a researcher at Johns Hopkins who is looking into the emotional components of heart attacks has found the actual spot in the brain that connects the emotions to the heartbeat. Stephen M. Oppenheimer, a neurological researcher, says that the spot in the brain that controls the heartbeat is linked up with the emotional portion of the brain known as the limbic nervous system.

Because of this link the very core of a person's health is affected by such emotions as anger, fear, sadness, and loneliness. This even explains why healthy people in some cultures die of voodoo curses. "If you truly believe that you are going to die because someone told you so, then that becomes a tremendous, unresolvable stress," said Oppenheimer in *The Wall Street Journal*.

Oppenheimer's research also goes a long way toward explaining why prayer, which most people find comforting, has the power to heal patients recovering from surgery. At the very least prayer soothes the uneasy heart.

Although Oppenheimer's research shows the physiological connection between such things as prayer and health, it doesn't explain some excellent studies by hospitals that show that heart attack patients recover faster even if strangers pray for them *without their knowledge*. How can that be explained?

One such study was published in the *Southern Medical Journal* and was conducted by Dr. Randolph Bird, a cardiologist at the University of California at San Francisco. He took four hundred patients who had either had or were suspected of having had heart attacks. This group was divided in half, with both receiving state-of-the-art medical care.

One group, however, was prayed for. These prayer sessions were conducted without the knowledge of the group. Brief biographical sketches were prepared of the patients using first names only. These sketches were given to Protestant and Catholic prayer groups, who were asked to pray for these people.

The results were astounding. None of the prayed-for patients died, fewer had to have resuscitation, and as a group they needed fewer antibiotics and drugs for heart failure. Results like this show that if prayer were a pill, it would be ordered routinely in our hospitals.

Initially I had doubts about this study. How could people be helped by prayers they didn't even know were being said for them? It didn't make sense. I decided to test it in my own office.

Although I am not particularly religious and do not feel comfortable praying for my patients, I have an office nurse who does. She routinely prays for my hospitalized patients.

So I examined hospital audits of my patients that were conducted by outside auditors who routinely assess physician performance. These audits take into consideration the illness, type of patient, and any complications they might have. Since ours is a teaching hospital, all patients receive virtually the same treatment from the residents. What I discovered was that my patients go home from the hospital one to two days earlier than the Washington State average.

Does that mean prayer is responsible for more rapid healing? Could it be true that the prayers of my office nurse are largely responsible for the fact that my patients spend $200,000 a year less on hospitalization than the Washington State average?

I don't know the answers, but I will say this: Before I began studying mystical experiences such as death-related visions, I thought that they were just neurochemically inspired fantasies. Now I realize that they are just some of the wonderful mysteries that surround us on a daily basis. These mysteries are not hidden from sight. They are in plain view for anyone who looks for them.

5

THE SECRET CLUB

Just because man has a need to see God
doesn't mean there isn't one.

—Glen Gabbard

When I first published work on near-death experiences, I expected to receive ridicule and outright hostility from my peers. I was afraid that my work would be seen as an attempt to prove life after death, or as being too much in "the Twilight Zone" to be acceptable. I wasn't prepared for what happened. Instead of being ostracized, I suddenly found myself to be a member of what feels like a secret club. The unstated aim of this "club" is to add knowledge and understanding to medicine that isn't currently there.

I don't know how many caregivers are in this club, since there is no official membership list, but I do know that the numbers are large and becoming larger. If the "members" with whom I have been in contact are any gauge, this club is peopled by some of the very best and brightest medicine has to offer. They are the ones who have learned the most about modern medicine and know its capabilities and its limitations.

These caregivers are not at "Guru U" or some new-age institute. They are at established and respected medical centers, such as Chicago Children's Hospital, Toledo Medical Center, and Miami Children's Hospital, and are in positions of power and authority. Disturbed by a medical world that sometimes seems to be concerned only with expensive technology, they are quietly attempting to renew the spirit of medicine.

I did not discover this secret club on my own, it discovered me. After I published my studies on near-death experiences and children, I began to hear from my colleagues, some of them the most respected names in medicine. Usually they would call me on the telephone late at night, when they were unwinding and reflecting on the practice of medicine. These were the same people I saw in the hallways at the hospital or sat next to at pediatric conferences. In those settings we never discussed spiritual issues, but the nighttime telephone calls were different. They contained firsthand accounts of spiritual visions from people who work with death and dying on a daily basis.

"I KNOW WHAT HAPPENS AFTER DEATH"

One such story comes from Dr. Clifton Furukawa, an internationally recognized allergist as well as a compassionate clinician. He has written textbooks and medical-journal articles that have been responsible for many of the advances in pediatrics. I spent six months working with him in his allergy clinic at Seattle Children's Hospital and have discussed many difficult cases of asthma with him.

Still I knew little about his personal life. So I was unprepared for the late-night telephone call I received from him in which he told me about the out-of-body experience he had had in relationship to his son's death.

In a calm and clinical manner Furukawa told me about the pain of watching his son drown at a lake in Washington State. He dove into the water to save the boy, when suddenly he felt as though he was out of his physical body, watching himself. The scene was extremely real and vivid, so vivid in fact that he could see the hairs on the top of his own head and even look around at the mountains and the water.

He felt completely at peace and emotionally detached as, from this puzzling vantage point, he watched himself struggle. "At this point I had the sort of empathy that one might feel with a patient," he told me. "I felt sorry about what I was seeing, yet I really had no feelings."

As he watched himself, he became aware that there was a being behind him "watching the two mes."

Furukawa had a sense that he would die if his struggle continued. As he considered this option, the spirit spoke to him without actually speaking, conveying to him that he had a choice to continue until he died or to return to his body, which would then be in great emotional agony. He chose to return.

"It was the worst emotional pain I have ever experienced," he told me.

Through the pain of losing his son, Furukawa experienced some positive changes. For one thing he now has a greatly decreased fear of death. He also sees a greater meaning to life. "Since the death of my son I think I know what happens when we die," he told me. "That knowledge has been a relief."

Furukawa shared his story with me as a confirmation that I was examining something important. I should not have any doubts about researching spiritual matters, he said. Rather I should proceed as boldly as possible.

Furukawa's experience gave me the courage to continue in my research. I had already learned so much from him as a physician. Now I became aware that one can be a hard-nosed scientist and a mystic.

"IT WAS GOING TO HAPPEN SOON"

Another such caregiver is Rosemarie Guadagnini, a senior nurse who has spent a lifetime practicing her profession and researching it for nursing journals.

As a first-year nursing student she had her first experience of the extraordinary degree of insight that many people who are dying demonstrate. She was assisting during a routine medical procedure on a Muslim man who was in his mid-forties. When he was placed on the operating table, he asked which way his head was facing. When told it was facing west, he calmly told the nurses and doctor that it had to be facing east or he would die.

His position was changed. But during surgery the position became inconvenient for the doctor performing the operation, and the table was rotated back to its original position. Within minutes the man died.

An autopsy was unable to reveal a cause of death. He had no hidden disease, no unexpected bleeding, no signs of shock, and no heart attack.

This puzzling episode was the first to give Rosemarie the

idea that patients can perceive the possibility of their own death and may even have some control over it.

There were other such episodes. At one time she cared for a young mother who had just given birth to a healthy infant. Unexpectedly the mother began to insist that she was going to die. Immediately she began to plan for her death, relaying her wishes for the baby to the appropriate people.

Her feelings were not ignored by her doctors. Her physician took this very seriously, and she was examined by a number of specialists.

"I asked her how she knew she was going to die, and she said she didn't know," said Rosemarie. "But she was certain that it was going to happen soon."

This was in the early 1950s, when women spent several days in bed after giving birth. When they got her out of bed on the fourth day, a blood clot moved into her lungs and killed her.

These experiences happened early in Rosemarie's career and helped shape it. They taught her never to ignore what a patient is telling her.

She heard near-death experiences from patients, long before Dr. Raymond Moody's research gave them a name. She also found that the words *parting visions* can be widely defined. Sometimes patients who were going to die saw a woman in white who would tell them of their impending death. Other times, though, patients would merely have intuitions that something dreadful was going to happen. She always listened to these messages, no matter how they were transmitted to the patients.

In one case a death-related vision came through a drawing.

"I Am Going to a Special Place"

The drawing was produced by a little boy named Toby. He was three years old when he checked into the hospital where Rosemarie worked in New York City. He was in remission from leukemia and was in the hospital for a checkup.

One day in the playroom he began to tell Rosemarie about a recent dream. The dream, he said, told a story about a trip. Curious, she asked him to draw a picture of it. With crayons he drew a picture that was dark blue and gray on the left side. On the right he drew pictures of yellow and white flowers, bright blue birds, and a variety of pets.

"Pretty soon I am going to a special place," he said when the drawing was finished. On his way to the special place, Toby said, he would first have to pass through a world of darkness, which he pointed to in the left-hand side of his drawing. It wasn't scary, though, he told Rosemarie, especially since he knew the beauty that was waiting on the other side.

"When are you going there?" asked Rosemarie.

"I don't know for sure," he told her. "But it is going to be soon, and I'll like it there."

Within a week Toby died.

Lessons Learned and Used

Experiences like these taught Rosemarie that there is more to a patient than the medical record. Another experience showed her that the spoken word can affect a patient's spiritual and physical outcome as much as the most powerful medicine.

Early in her career she attended a patient named Mona, a thirty-two-year-old mother of three with a brain tumor. Although much of the tumor had been removed, the surgeons could not get it all. Since it was malignant and in a deep spot in the brain, it was quite clear that she was not going to be alive much longer.

Unaware of the bad prognosis, she still held hope for her own recovery. Then one morning, when Rosemarie was in the room, a harried neurosurgeon came into the room with Mona's chart. He got right to the point. "Mona, in about another week you will be dead," he said. Then he turned and walked out.

Mona and her husband began to cry. So did Rosemarie. She tried to console the couple but found that it was to no avail, since she could barely contain her own emotions. She left the room and went on with her duties.

Within an hour of the doctor's visit Mona was in a coma. Two hours later she died.

This display of insensitivity along with the many inspiring moments experienced in Rosemarie's career have underscored for her the need for compassion and understanding when dealing with the terminally ill. She has helped many patients face death, just as she has helped many of them understand their parting visions. She has used this knowledge in her own life as well.

When her cousin was dying, he became wild and uncontrollable. He was gravely ill and agitated by a high fever, but most of all he did not want to die. By the time Sharon arrived, her cousin had been restrained with straps and catheterized.

She didn't want other family members to see him in that condition. Most of all she did not want him to die that way.

"I went to the bed and said, quite strongly, 'Kenneth, stop it and be still. I am going to take all this stuff off, and then you and I will talk.' "

As she unstrapped him, she talked about the days when she

used to live by the beach in California and he would visit her. Pulling close to his ear, she reminded him of how he used to lie in the sun and gaze at the distant horizon.

"Imagine yourself there right now," she whispered, verbally painting a picture of the warm beach and the sunny blue sky.

As he calmed down, she talked about the death that was ahead of him. She wrote to me in a letter what she said: "Take a little rest and put yourself on the beach blanket. You are starting a journey that takes a lot of energy, so rest. When you are ready, we will begin. We're all here, and we will all be walking with you and sharing our love and energy, but when we come to the gate, then you must go alone. You're the only one who can open the gate. On the other side of the gate will be permanent light and love, and guess who will meet you?"

He smiled and said, "Daddy and Grandpa." For the next few hours Rosemarie and other members of the family drew close and talked to the dying man. Finally he slipped calmly away.

The veteran nurse had learned her lessons well. After years of watching and learning, she was so confident in her spirituality that she was able to turn a potential disaster into a "good death."

DOCTORS FIGHT FOR CONTROL

The concept of a "good death" is a difficult one for most physicians. Death is the doctor's enemy, the thing we fight against. We are taught that when it wins, we lose. I, too, believe this to be true and certainly fight against death as hard as anyone else in my profession. Yet this determined battle against the Grim

Reaper leads to a certain amount of denial, both by health care workers and by those who use the health care system. A neurosurgeon at Detroit Children's Hospital showed it best when I asked her if she had ever witnessed death-related experiences with her patients: "No way," she said. "My patients don't die."

She laughed and went on to give me a more serious answer. Yet there was a lot of truth in the surgeon's joke, a truth that is important in understanding how doctors and nurses think about death-related visions. Research has shown that beneath the brusque attitude and callous manner of many health care workers lurks a deep longing to understand the spiritual dimension that exists within each of us.

One such physician is Dr. Goren Grip. A Swedish anesthesiologist, he is a lecturer and practitioner at a major university hospital in Sweden. He is an excellent doctor with an added edge that most physicians don't have: When he was a child, Grip had a near-death experience. This experience has had a tremendous effect upon the way he practices medicine.

At the age of five he was admitted to the hospital for a minor surgical procedure. The anesthesiologist gave young Grip too much ether, which caused a brief respiratory failure and a possible cardiac arrest. With that, Grip had an experience that has influenced virtually everything he has done in his life.

As he lay on the operating table, he saw a being of light on a road in front of him. He felt a strong love emitted from the being, followed by a review of his short life. There were no sounds or words accompanying this review, only strong images.

"I re-experienced everything that had happened in my life and watched it as a spectator with the being," says Grip. "Most of what I saw was about me and my brother, of whom I was very jealous. My attention was focused on our exchanges of emotions, my jealousy, my feelings of triumph when I hit him, his surprise when I hit him for no reason, his anger and resentment, and later his triumph when he got back at me."

Grip also experienced the few loving moments he had with his brother. "When I did something loving to him, I experienced my love, my brother's surprise, as well as his love and happiness. I experienced his feelings as clearly as my own, making this a fantastic lesson on the consequences of my own actions. It was the love from the being of light that gave me the strength to see my life exactly as it was, without making it better or worse."

Grip was profoundly transformed by his experience. The message of unconditional love and giving that he received from his encounter with the being of light is what led him to become a doctor.

It doesn't matter if the experience was just a crazy dream or caused by lack of oxygen to the brain, says Grip. "What does matter is that I received knowledge about the meaning of life in this experience. After having spent years testing this knowledge I can see that it is valid, meaningful, and durable. Because of that it doesn't really matter how I came to get it."

Despite the positive aspects of his near-death experience, Grip knows firsthand the professional difficulties of discussing his vision too freely. As he wryly states, "I have had the typical problems of someone who is transformed but is living in a world which is not."

The world he is talking about is the scientific one, in which his fellow physicians have used his spiritual experience to ridicule him. Grip is tolerant of this ridicule. Some of it, he says, is academic infighting and can be ignored. But some of the ridicule goes deeper than that.

"Understanding something like the human body gives doctors a sense of control over it," says Grip. "So when we encounter something that we can't explain, there is a chance that our worldview might collapse. That is why so many doctors laugh at spiritual experiences. They are really afraid of them."

Grip meets far less ridicule from patients, although he is careful about broaching the subject of the childhood experience that shaped his life, since years of medical practice have taught him that not every patient wants to discuss the spiritual aspects of death. "I never force my experience on anyone," says Grip. "I have learned the hard way never to force such a powerful experience on someone who is not ready for it."

A fine example of what Grip is talking about is the time he was asked to talk to a patient who was dying of liver cancer. Rather than tell the man the hard and cold facts of his illness, Grip spoke very few words. He told the patient his name and then said, "So, they have told you that you have liver cancer. What do you know about that?"

As the man spoke, Grip could see the pain in the man's eyes. Rather than pressure him to talk, Grip sat in silence, even tying his shoes so as to give the man the chance to avoid eye contact as he talked about his illness.

After rambling for some time the man began talking about the course his disease would take and finally about death itself. When they finished and Grip had told him everything he could about death and its spiritual aspects, the man thanked him. "You know, that was a tough discussion," he said. "But it was much better talking to you than to a doctor."

Grip told the man that he was in fact a medical doctor. The man was quite embarrassed, but Grip was complimented by the sense that this man found him warm and caring. He knew that he had made the best of a volatile situation.

"When you are trying to help someone gain a painful insight, you must never go ahead of him and point the way, or he will stop listening to you," says Grip. "Instead he must be allowed to make this inner tour at his own pace. You have to follow lightly and with a keen ear in order not to disturb him. Ultimately the only thing you can do is offer security and protection for his thoughts."

HAPPENINGS THAT DEFY BELIEF

"Security and protection for his thoughts." Since most caregivers, physicians especially, are trained to ignore such things as death-related visions, then the very least we can do is offer security and protection for a patient's thoughts. All that really amounts to is listening, and there is no reason to object to that.

It is important to note that the medical literature is full of death-related visions that are witnessed by doctors and nurses regardless of their spiritual beliefs. Many of these visions have even happened to caregivers firsthand. In fact it could easily be said that in many cases doctors and nurses have these experiences despite their beliefs.

NURSES' SENSITIVITY
TO THE SPIRITUAL

Anthropologist David Lewis randomly interviewed 108 nurses at a London hospital. He found that 35 percent reported having experiences with dead patients. These ranged from vague feelings of their presence to outright visual and auditory experiences.

One such experience, reported in a British journal, *Nursing Times,* involved the frequent sighting of a fourteen-year-old boy who had died in a surgical ward. Here is a nurse's report of her encounter:

I'm not a person who believes in ghosts, but while working in a male surgical ward in an old hospital in Sunderland, I was sitting writing up the report cards when I heard someone calling, "Nurse."

I looked up and saw what I thought was a woman in a long white nightie, but then I put it down to being a fourteen-year-old boy who'd just come back from theater [surgery] and still had the theater gown on.

I finished the sentence I was on and then went to investigate. I got as far as the sluice and I thought I felt something or someone going back the other way, and out of the corner of my eye I again thought I saw something or someone dressed all in white.

I went to check the boys [in the ward], but they were fast asleep. Then as I was going back down the corridor, I felt and thought I saw something white again pass me. . . .

Later I went for a tea break, and a nurse who had been in a different ward at the bottom of the same corridor as the ward I was on came and flopped in a chair. . . . She'd had more or less exactly the same experience.

Lewis has done his work at the Alister Hardy Research Center at Nottingham University, which has collected more than five thousand accounts of spiritual experiences. He has concluded that caregivers are "sensitized" to visionary encounters because the work they do involves so many death-related crises.

VISIONS REPORTED BY DOCTORS

A number of studies have shown that in the weeks before death, dying patients consistently have vivid visions of deceased relatives and another world.

Pediatric oncologist Diane Komp, of Yale, reported children who had dreams or visions before their death. These visions open up a dialogue on the child's impending death that is beneficial to both the patients and those around them.

For example, an eight-year-old boy who was dying of cancer had parents who avoided the discussion of death. All that changed when the boy had a vision of Jesus. He said that a big yellow school bus had parked in front of his house, and Jesus invited him aboard, telling him he was going to die soon.

Komp tells about another boy who was dying of central-nervous-system leukemia. She thought the boy was on the verge of dying. Then one afternoon he told her that God had spoken to him and he asked God if he could live another year so that he could explain his death to his three-year-old brother.

Komp thought that such a lengthy survival would be medically impossible. Yet the boy in fact did survive another year.

Hundreds of cases similar to these have been reported in the medical literature.

SCIENCE OF FAITH

Cases like these were summed up in one respect by Dr. William Osler, one of the founders of modern medicine, who said, "Faith is the great mover of mankind, and yet cannot be measured on the laboratory scales."

Yet despite the presence of these cases in the medical literature, it is easy to find insensitivity in medicine. At times it is almost as though the profession demands it.

Caregiving is a difficult and demanding job that can try even the most saintly of doctors and nurses. At times the pressure to "process" patients becomes so great that the last thing even a very caring doctor wants to do is spend time helping a patient figure out the meaning of a vision.

There are other factors as well, ones that can be summed up by an old adage: "What makes a person good at some things makes him bad at others." That is certainly true of caregivers. This is a profession that has deep and thick roots in science. And science in turn is rooted deeply in skepticism. And skepticism is rooted deeply in proof and more proof. "Show me the data" is what my medical-school professors used to say. "Give me the proof."

Of course that is what medical science has to be. But the medical literature is full of "proof" about death-related visions. As you can see from the bibliography of this book alone, there are reams of solid medical analyses available to any physician with curiosity about the visionary aspects of dying.

It really is not lack of proof or data that keeps most physicians from being sensitive about these experiences. Could it be fear of criticism? To some extent yes. I have found that the most cynical person tends to be the most verbal in a group. I have found that it isn't uncommon to have my research attacked by a cynic only to have others in a discussion group lend it their full support when the cynical person is no longer around. I have found that the great majority of clinicians have deep spiritual beliefs yet choose to keep quiet about them. This fear of criticism keeps some caregivers quiet when they should actually be most vocal.

The fear of lack of control is another likely cause of insen-

sitivity surrounding these death-related visions. Medical training and care are about control. If you ever doubt this, note how
many times the vital signs of a person in the hospital are monitored. Blood pressure, body temperature, urine output, and
heart rate are all the stuff of medical charts.

Death-related visions come unexpectedly. Physicians and
nurses cannot control their arrival or departure, and therefore
they often fear them the way a homeowner might fear an intruder. All doctors and nurses can do is try to explain them (if
they have read the data) or call them names, such as "hallucinations" or "bad dreams."

Loss of control is frightening for anyone, but for doctors and
nurses it is more so because it can be equated with failure.

I know all of the factors that can lead to insensitivity in medicine because I have been guilty of it myself at times. In fact I
could point to others in looking for examples of this most glar-
ing shortcoming of my profession, but I think it is fairer to examine one of my own failures of sensitivity.

A MISTAKE OF MY OWN

When I was a resident, a young man was brought into the
emergency room with a serious head injury from an automobile accident. In a short period of time it was quite obvious that
he was brain-dead.

I was cocky and young and thought I knew it all. I felt that
the thing a truly in-control doctor should do was to tell this
boy's mother the reality of her son's condition. I soon found
out that it was a little more reality than she wanted to chew.

Without backing into the subject at all, I answered this

woman's question about her son. When she asked me what was going to happen to him, I abruptly told her that he would probably remain just the way he was, in a vegetative state.

She became furious and told the medical director of the hospital that I had called her son a "vegetable," who would "spend the rest of his life in a nursing home." None of that was true, and at the time I could not figure out why she had misinterpreted what I had said. Now I understand. I should have tried to learn what she knew of her son's condition, asking her at least a little bit about her fears instead of being so blunt with my medical-book predictions. Something the medical director said to me sums up what's at the root of much of the insensitivity in medicine: "Sometimes book learning doesn't replace just being human."

Indeed I should have just listened to her and talked with her about her fears. After all, if I could not just talk to this parent about her feelings, then how could I ever hope to hear something so important as another person's spiritual experience? Since then I have learned that such mothers often know the answers to their own questions. My explanations were not needed. My silence was.

Fortunately more and more physicians are willing to recognize the important role that faith and spirituality play for many of their patients. When the subject comes up, they are not afraid to admit that medicine does not know everything. They are willing to let their patients in on the scientific debate over spiritual experiences and to let them make up their own minds.

Sometimes these caregivers have even had spiritual experiences themselves.

"I WANT TO TAKE A
BIG BITE OUT OF LIFE"

One such physician was the late Dr. John Jones, of Davis, California. As a bomber pilot during World War II, Jones had a near-death experience that puzzled him for years before he learned what it was that had happened. It also transformed him and led him into a practice of medicine that had him caring for many who could not afford medical care.

As he told his wife about the experience, "I have had a vision, I don't know what else to call it. I will never be afraid to die." As a result he was clearly never afraid to live either. Here is his story:

While flying in formation in the lead B-24 bomber in his squadron, Jones's airplane suddenly heeled to the right and went into a spin. He passed through other bombers flying below him, coming dangerously close to collision. At last there was nothing below him but the deep blue of the Mediterranean Sea.

He pulled back on the controls, but the airplane did not respond. Down it went, plummeting toward the water. Jones was sure he was going to die. As the acceleration increased, he took his hands off the controls and was pressed against the seat. Surely this was the end of his life.

Suddenly he had the sensation of passing through a long tunnel. At the end of the tunnel was a brilliant light, and a person standing in it. He knew that the person in that light was Jesus. He felt a deep sense of peace and well-being. Later he told his wife that he never wanted to leave this place.

Then, as suddenly as it began, he found himself back in his

body and in the airplane. It had somehow righted itself and was flying low and steady over the water.

The experience had a great effect on Jones. After graduating from the University of Tennessee Medical School, he settled in the Sacramento Valley in California.

He helped found the Haight-Ashbury Free Clinic in the 1960s in San Francisco. Then, along with two nonmedical friends, he started a free clinic in Davis that included women's and children's services, a dental clinic, and a midwifery program. His main concern as a doctor was for those he called the medically underserved.

When John Jones died of cancer in 1991, a local newspaper columnist wrote that "the underdog never had a better friend than John Jones." He received several awards for humanitarian service, and one that is given annually in the Sacramento area bears his name.

I never met Jones. His wife, Nancy, wrote to me to say that my books about near-death experiences explained why her husband worked so hard to make a better life for others. She also described his last days as he died of cancer.

"He died peacefully at home, in his own bed, with myself and two of our children at his side. He seemed anxious to go and for several days had been asking me, 'Do you think we're getting close?' I know he was not afraid to die. He had often said to me, 'I want to take a big bite out of life,' and death was a further adventure."

"MY LIFE WILL NEVER BE THE SAME"

Another caregiver whose approach to life has been changed by a death-related vision is Catherine Clark, a physical therapist in Oregon.

She comes from a close family in Eugene with deep roots in the area. Her grandfather Dr. Robert D. Clark was formerly president of the University of Oregon.

At the age of eighty-five Catherine's grandmother slipped into a coma. She had been fighting cancer for several months and was now in intense pain from radiation and chemotherapy. The doctors said that they had done everything they could for the grandmother and that the family should prepare itself for the inevitable. Opal Ruth Clark was going to die.

The family made some tough decisions. They opted to keep her at home and to set up shifts for her care. In a family meeting they decided to avoid any attempts at resuscitation and told her physicians that visits would no longer be necessary. They made arrangements with a hospice to receive visits from a home-care nurse. Preparations were made for cremation, which is what the grandmother wanted.

For the next two weeks the family took loving care of their grandmother. Although she was in a coma, they always assumed that she could hear them and knew what was going on. Every two hours they turned her and checked for signs of skin breakdown. In between they talked and read to her. A couple of times a day they massaged her with rose milk.

They never lied to her about her condition, just as they didn't conceal their sadness about losing her.

After two weeks the grandmother woke up. She opened her

eyes at four in the morning and asked for a drink of water. Catherine was there and was shocked. She gave her grandmother a water-soaked sponge and watched her gratefully "wet her whistle." Then as she rapidly came out of it, the grandmother told Catherine things that, as Catherine put it, "sent warm electric shocks up my spine."

In a letter Catherine wrote to me she told of this conversation with her grandmother:

She spoke of a tunnel of light, which she insisted was hovering just feet above her bed. She gave eerily accurate details of who cared for her while she was in a coma and remembered several specific conversations as well as specific poems and Bible passages that were read to her. She thanked me for setting her hair and applying lipstick, an activity I did several times just before she had old friends visit to say their good-byes. She remembered her sister, Jeanne, being at her bedside, which in fact she was for two days — but at that time Grandma was in a deep coma and was completely unresponsive.

One night the whole family gathered at her bedside and we ate dinner there and talked about Grandma and all the wonderful things she had done for each one of us. The night we all gathered together, Grandma was still in a coma, yet later she recalled us all being there. She said that a man came into the room leading a gray horse and that all of us just kept talking while she tried to get our attention because she wanted us to tell him to leave, that horses weren't allowed inside. Finally she told the man to leave herself, and he did. When Grandma told us of this experience, I watched my mother's face go white with shock.

Since her "awakening" my grandmother has had visitations from another man, not the same one who led the horse. This man has been an important source of comfort to her, and in fact since his appearing, my grandma has had no pain. We stopped giving her oral morphine. She has been fully oriented to the present with no real signs of dementia and no medications to sedate her for four full days, yet she experiences as part of her reality a comforting spirit, which none of us can see or hear. She says he's tall and dark but has given him no name; she refers to him as "the man." She stubbornly refuses to say much about him except that he is there waiting to take her home. I have watched her from a distance, and at times she appears to be talking and reaching out to someone; yet there is nothing there that I can sense personally.

Catherine and her family feel lucky to have shared this experience. It helped them move through their grief and, as she put it, "rejoice in her life and in her passing despite the fact that we love her and will miss her terribly."

This experience with her grandmother has had a profound effect on the way Catherine approaches her job and her patients too. She summed it up nicely in her letter:

> For the last six years I have worked in an acute setting in a hospital and I have faced death many times. But now I see death in a different light and I look forward to moving ahead and assisting others who are struggling with their fears and misconceptions. I do believe there is a place for both science and spirit and that each is not necessarily separate from the other. Together they are quality patient care.

SPIRIT AND MEDICINE

Are doctors creating false hope by acknowledging the spiritual side of human beings? Should we leave discussion of such things up to ministers and chaplains and stick with our pills and tests? Is it fraudulent for a doctor to offer hope through spiritual pathways?

I don't know the answer to those questions. But I do know that we physicians do not have to tell our patients lies or delude them with cultural myths as part of a spiritual dialogue. At the very least we should let them in on this very exciting scientific debate and allow them to have the true facts about death-related visions. Only then can we erase cynicism and permit true skepticism, which is simply the ability to question all things but believe that all things are possible.

Physicians do not have to turn into ministers. There are many physicians who attend to the needs of the human spirit as they do their jobs of physical healing.

One such physician is Dr. Sapathy Silva, head of cardiothoracic surgery at Toronto General Hospital. When asked about the human spirit by patients, Silva tells them the simple scientific truth: There is a vital element in our anatomy that has the ability to see our body and the world around it while it is clinically dead. He points out that the physical body cannot see or feel this vital element, but it is there.

Silva does not go so far as to say that this element is proof of life after death. He is simply restating what physicians have said since the beginning of medicine: The spirit of human beings needs attention too.

Listening to that spirit is often as important as pills and surgery.

6

GUIDED BY
THE LIGHT

Every part of the body has a story to tell.

—Anna Halprin

Death-related visions give us insight into what our own death will be like and teach us meaningful lessons on how to live.

Few stories illustrate this notion more perfectly than the visionary events in the life of a nursing-home worker I'll call Martha.

Martha was always very close to her mother. When Martha divorced her husband, she moved into a house next door to her mother. Between the two of them they raised Martha's four children. The mother never complained about this sort of "second motherhood" that had taken place. Instead she enjoyed caring for the children during the day while her daughter was at work.

One day, quite unexpectedly, the mother died. She had a heart attack and was dead before the paramedics arrived.

Martha felt destroyed by the loss. She stayed home from her job until her finances forced her to return to work. Even then she kept her mother's house just as it was when she died and would visit it daily. "Her spirit was still there," she explained. "And it felt good to just have that presence around."

About a year after the mother's death two of Martha's children were killed in an automobile accident. They were riding in a car with one of their uncles when another car made a left turn in front of them. The children were thrown through the windshield and died en route to the hospital.

Martha was devastated, and so was the rest of the family. These children had been the "babies" of the family, and their unexpected loss was as painful as the loss of Martha's mother.

It seemed as though the only one in the family who could maintain composure was Martha. She selected the caskets and arranged the funeral. She even planned the service and helped the minister write the eulogy. She did this all alone, with no family help, mainly because she was the only one in the family who could control her emotions.

The day before the funeral she went to her children's closet and selected their best Sunday outfits. Then she went to the funeral home, where she was given a private room in which to dress them for burial. The children's bodies were brought into the room, and then she was left alone.

Martha undressed her children and looked at their bodies one last time. She realized now that she had held her emotions in for too long. She began to sob.

Suddenly she noticed that her mother was standing in the room next to her. She was smiling as she placed a comforting hand on her daughter.

"It's okay," she said to Martha. "They are here with me now. I'll take care of them."

This vision at this time was like a spiritual rebirth for Martha. She had lost so much in the past year, but in just these few seconds it was behind her.

"When my mother appeared to me, I suddenly understood everything," said Martha. "I knew what would happen when I died and I knew what my goal on earth should be."

For Martha that goal is to help other people, especially those in need of spiritual renewal. As a direct result of this vision she now works in nursing homes as a nursing assistant. She takes great pride in working with people who are very senile or dying. Jobs like these are among the most challenging in society. Such work involves extremely difficult tasks, such as feeding people who are too old to swallow well, or changing diapers for those who are too feeble to leave their bed. These occupations have a very high burnout rate. Yet Martha has done this type of job for more than twenty years now and says she would be completely comfortable doing it for twenty more.

It is the vision she had of her mother that keeps her going. She feels that it is her job to relay to the sick and dying what she has seen.

"I tell these old people my own story," she said. "It helps them feel good about their own lives and takes away their fears of dying."

FEARLESS LIVING

Martha's story serves to illustrate a hard fact of death-related visions. Not only do they hint at answers to the question of life after death, they also give us the knowledge that our lives are significant, important, and filled with meaning.

Not only people who actually experience death-related visions but even those who only hear about them receive these benefits as well. A study conducted by psychologist Vernon Larson proves this point.

He has studied the effects of death-related visions on the lives of people who simply read about them. To do this, he administered death-anxiety tests to dozens of people before having them read literature on death-related visions. Several days after the test subjects had read the material, Larson administered the tests again. He found that 87 percent of his subjects had an increased belief in life after death, an increase in the desire to love others, and an increase in the desire to demonstrate love to others. His subjects made such comments about death-related visions as "confirms my faith" and "gives me a new understanding of death."

There are other studies that show the positive power of just knowing about death-related visions. Dr. Bruce Greyson, while a doctor of emergency psychiatry at the University of Connecticut, gave literature on near-death experiences to a number of patients who had attempted suicide. Along with this literature he also administered the usual psychiatric treatment for those who attempt suicide. To another, control group he just administered the usual medical treatment and did not include the literature.

Greyson found that very few of those who read about these death-related visions attempt to kill themselves again. On the other hand those who didn't read about them tried to commit suicide again with the usual frequency, an astounding fifty to one hundred times the rate of the normal population.

I have seen the hope that death-related visions provide my own patients as well as many of the people in my studies. I also hear reports from other health care workers of the hope, compassion, and understanding that they provide. As a result I have attempted to articulate a number of ways in which death-related visions affect us all:

- Death-related visions validate the intuitions and even visions that all of us have in our ordinary waking lives.
- Death-related visions demonstrate that there is a large area of the human brain that is underutilized. This area contains paranormal abilities that are rarely used by humans and is often activated during death and near death.
- Death-related visions give us insight into what our own death will be like and even show us how to live life to its fullest. For example, people who have had near-death experiences are more relaxed about life because they have less fear of death.
- These spiritual experiences can act as cultural icebreakers to begin a new dialogue about spirituality. As a result many of our institutions are likely to change, including medicine and what can reasonably be expected from it.

A SIMPLE MESSAGE BROUGHT HOME

Very little is known about how afraid most of us actually are of death. Some psychologists argue that death anxiety is at the root of all human fears. They even go so far as to say that death anxiety leads directly to our use of deodorants, our obsession with youth, and even our illusory sense of security in the possession of nuclear weapons. Other psychologists argue that we cannot even conceive of our own deaths and therefore do not fear it at all.

These are all big theories with little scientific evidence to back them up. But there is one truth that I can attest to: Listening to death-related visions gives us profound insight into how to live our lives.

The message is a clear and simple one that we have just forgotten over the years: Death is not to be feared, and life is to be lived to the fullest.

Death-related visions just bring this message home again.

EQUIPPED FOR VISIONS

One of the many things proven by death-related visions is that our brain is equipped to have spiritual visions.

In fact, death-related visions shatter forever the notion that human beings do not have a spiritual side. They are proof that paranormal abilities are not the creation of con men and hucksters but are real events that happen to real people.

I think that in the future our generation will be ridiculed for its refusal to believe in and develop its paranormal abilities. Rather than learning how to utilize this fascinating aspect of the human brain, we have let skeptics guide our thinking. Many of these skeptics have never conducted any scientific studies on such paranormal occurrences as death-related visions, but they denigrate their importance and reality just the same.

A scientific study that proves my point was published in the *British Medical Journal.* It examined cases of miraculous cures, in which patients had been declared to be terminally ill by doctors yet were cured by visionary experiences and/or prayer.

The study didn't examine the miracle cures themselves. Rather it examined the response of the medical establishment to them. The researchers found that as soon as a miracle cure was documented, the physicians involved in the cases immediately began to discredit the original diagnosis. They did not want to lend credence to anything spiritual, even though there was overwhelming evidence that a spiritual event had at least contributed to the cure.

A CASE OF SPIRITUAL HEALING

I had just such a case of a possible spiritual healing in my own practice. When I was conducting Teryn Hedlund's two-month physical examination, I noticed that she had a hernia of her ovary. I referred her to Children's Hospital for routine surgery to repair the tear. But when surgeons operated on her, they found that her liver was enlarged and her abdomen was filled with fluid.

Specialists in liver diseases were consulted, and she was diagnosed as having a variant of Wolman's disease, a defect in the way the body processes fat. With Wolman's disease abnormal fat deposits are laid down throughout the body, especially in the liver, until this vital organ clogs up and ceases to function. A liver transplant is no help, since a new liver will quickly be affected.

The diagnosis was confirmed by several specialists after biopsies were taken and slides were examined a number of ways, including by electron microscopy. There was no doubt that Teryn had a severe metabolic disease.

This was a heartbreaking situation. This child was going to die, and I had to tell the parents about it.

Two days before Christmas I told the parents the bad news. I cried as I explained the disease and why it was fatal. The picture before me was a grim one. The father, a rugged man with hands as tough as leather gloves, sobbed quietly as I offered the diagnosis. The mother fired questions rapidly, stunned that such a disease could have no effective treatment.

A few days later the parents wanted to talk to me. They were sure that Teryn's problems were due entirely to a formula that she had been given in the hospital. They wanted to know if they could try a new formula. I asked a metabolic expert at the hospital if a switch in formula was acceptable. He thought about it a moment and shrugged. "Mel, let them use any formula they want," he said. "The baby is going to die anyway."

But Teryn did not die. Instead she thrived. Week after week she gained weight. Her liver shrank and her skin color improved and could even be described as robust. By one year of age she had tripled her birth weight and was healthy against all odds.

I seemed to be seeing a miracle. Month after month she seemed healthier. After six months her liver had returned to normal size and the abdominal fluid had drained away. Teryn looked as normal as the other children in the waiting room.

I talked to the specialists who had handled Teryn's case, and they were just as astonished as I was. Her blood work was repeated, as were the liver biopsies, and all the tests came back normal. The same was true of the liver-enzyme tests. Somehow Teryn had healed.

I didn't understand this mysterious remission. If I had not been involved in this case personally, I would have assumed that the specialists somehow blew the diagnosis. But I knew the specialists involved. They were some of the nation's top experts in liver diseases, and the chance of their missing such an important call was a million to one. What had happened?

I knew from my near-death research that sometimes spiritual visions are associated with spontaneous cures. Had this happened? Indeed, Teryn's mother said that something baffling had happened on the day I had told them that their daughter was going to die. She said that her brother-in-law had heard a voice and acted on it and that maybe I should ask him about it. I called the brother-in-law, and he agreed to come in to the office and be interviewed. He described himself as not being a spiritual man and felt more comfortable at a party than in a church. Here is what he said:

I had been at work and came in around nine at night. I went into the bedroom and lay down to go to sleep. I was almost asleep when I heard a voice say, "Go to your niece's house and touch her abdomen."

I woke up completely and looked around. I could not really believe I had heard anything. The voice was loud and insistent, and I almost thought about getting up and doing what it told me to do, but I didn't. "I'll do it tomorrow," I said. I lay back down. Then the voice spoke up again. It said, "Go tonight. Tomorrow will be too late."

He immediately got out of bed and left the house. He did not tell his wife where he was going. He just got into his car and left, arriving at Teryn's house about ten o'clock.

Although he hadn't been to the house in several months, the

family thought he was there to lend emotional support and did not think it was terribly odd that he came by.

He asked if he could hold Teryn and then took her to another room. Mrs. Hedlund said, "Why are you doing this?" He replied, "I want to be alone with her, please." He put his hand on her abdomen as he had been told to do by the voice. The hand became warmer and warmer. He stayed there a few minutes and then abruptly left.

He later only told his father-in-law.

Was the brother-in-law's action the cause of Teryn's healing? I am inclined to think so. There is no ambiguity here, no symbols to interpret. The man heard a voice that caused him to jump out of bed and make a late-night journey to the bedside of his niece. He told his father-in-law about the voice before it was apparent Teryn would recover.

The coincidences are just too great for me to think that the brother-in-law's actions were not somehow associated with Teryn's outcome.

Luckily there are some researchers who can help me back up this point of view. They have examined these phenomena from many different angles. Some have collected and analyzed cases in which spiritual visions have led to the spontaneous healing of cancer. Others have risked the ridicule of their peer group by training that portion of their brain that has long been recognized as the point of origin for paranormal experiences. Still others have tapped into this area without even knowing it and have come away with astounding clinical results. I'll give you an example of each.

RESEARCH ON SPONTANEOUS HEALINGS

Arvin Gibson is an executive vice president for Utah Power and Light. His background is in nuclear engineering and he supervises more than sixteen hundred employees.

He is also a near-death researcher who has collected and examined hundreds of case studies dealing with death-related visions and their effects on the people who have them.

Gibson has documented several cases of spontaneous healings of cancer after spiritual visions. Because of his scientific background he knows the meaning of documentation, and since he is a religious person as well, he also knows that his work would be dismissed as biased if he didn't document it well.

One of the four cases he uncovered is of a woman named Anne. She was born and raised in Glendale, California, by parents who were Protestant, but not overly religious.

At the age of four Anne was diagnosed as having leukemia. She was hospitalized several times for evaluation of her blood, and many tests confirmed the diagnosis.

The spiritual vision that she credits with healing her leukemia took place when she was six years old. In itself the vision was quite extraordinary. Here is how she described it:

One night my mother put me to bed and tucked me in. I felt so tired and wanted to go to sleep, but suddenly I noticed a light coming into the room. It was a beautiful gold light, which seemed to appear on the left side of my bed. I wasn't afraid, I was just curious about the light. It was about three feet up in the air, and it grew in size. As the ball of light grew, the pain and the feeling of illness left me. I had no idea what was happening, but I was at peace.

I sat up and watched the light grow. It got so bright that it seemed the whole world was lit by it. I could see someone in the light. There was this beautiful woman, and she was part of the light, in fact she glowed. Her body was lit up inside in some way. It was hard to explain. It was like she was a crystal filled with light. Her feet were bare and she floated a few feet off the floor.

I had never felt such kindness and love. She called me by my name and held me to her. Communication was easy with her. All I did was think and she understood; it was some sort of mind thing.

Then the two of us moved through a short period of darkness, and we entered into an incredibly bright world, like nothing I had ever seen. I felt a deep peace and love. I had no idea where I was. The colors were bright and vibrant, beyond anything on this earth. I asked my guardian why she took me to this place. She said that I needed a rest, that life was very hard for me.

I played with some children in a play area on the grass with a sandbox. She came for me a little later and took me back through the darkness and back to my room. She said that it would be easier for me to live on earth now.

The next day this little girl was taken to the hospital for another round of tests. The tests puzzled her doctors because the leukemia was reversing itself. Over the next few days more tests showed that the disease was going away. Within two weeks Anne's blood tests were as normal as those of a person who had never even been suspected of having leukemia.

Is it possible to harness the powers of the mind to such an extent that we could induce healing visions? Or do they happen only the way Anne's did, unexpected and uninvited?

Gibson believes that these experiences represent God's method of communicating with human beings. If that were the case, it would make some area of the brain a receiver, capable of sensing spiritual messages. Gibson believes that there is an area of the brain that could indeed be made more sensitive with the appropriate training—such as meditation or prayer—but that the content of these visions is not under our control.

It could be an area of the brain vastly different from one that merely *generates* visions. It could mean that we are on the brink of discovering a whole other dimension of the mind.

BRAIN TRAINING AND HEALING

Regardless of what this area of the brain is, whether it is a generator of visions or a receiver of them, entire cultures have been built around developing the spiritual side of man.

Alexandra David-Neel wrote about Tibetan culture in the 1920s, before it was almost destroyed by the Communist Chinese. In her accounts the Tibetan monks spent many years developing the spiritual area of their brain in the same way that we spend years developing the left side of our brain by studying math and science.

Spiritually developed Tibetans were able to have out-of-body experiences and to visualize spiritual beings. They were also able to exercise complete mental control over their bodies, performing feats that seemed paranormal to others. For instance, many Tibetans were able to run for several days on end, covering great distances without tiring. They could even dry wet clothing by putting it on their backs and shivering so violently that their body heat would evaporate the water. They were also able to sit outside in the coldest of weather and stay warm through meditation.

Most of us would consider this paranormal, and indeed it was regarded as such for many years by Western observers. Then we came to realize that all of this could be done with training—mind over body, if you will. Where we spend years developing left-brain talents such as math and language, these people develop right-brain spiritual talents.

Feats such as those performed by Tibetan monks are still recognized as special but they are no longer considered paranormal. They are just the result of hard work and brain training.

That is how Dr. Kathi Kemper feels about being able to sense auras. Kemper is a medical doctor and was the director of the pediatric clinic at Harborview Hospital in Seattle, Washington. She describes herself as a left-brain person who excels in the left-brain world. She has published numerous articles in medical journals and is a courageous doctor in an inner-city hospital, where gunshot wounds are a common pediatric diagnosis.

Despite her obvious competence in medicine, Kemper reached a point where she felt limited by the type of medicine she was practicing. She felt that something was missing from her training that would keep her from being a complete healer. She feels that the way most physicians practice medicine is mechanistic. She wants to participate in the healing process, beyond prescribing medicines. She has technical knowledge, but wants to involve her own spirituality in the practice of medicine.

To do that, she took a course called "Therapeutic Touch." Although this sounds like a massage class, therapeutic touch actually proved to be a form of spiritual healing in which the healer's hands are passed a few inches over the patient's body and the person's aura is examined.

Kemper felt the course was scientifically sound. She saw parallels between therapeutic touch and such Chinese medical practices as acupuncture.

Kemper did not immediately learn how to sense auras. She practiced the techniques she had been taught, but she could never quite feel an aura.

Then one day she had a patient in the newborn nursery. She passed her hands about two or three inches over the infant's body before performing a more conventional hands-on examination and "saw" the child's aura.

"It was like the first time I ever heard a heart murmur with a stethoscope," she told me with great excitement. "It took me forever to finally hear a murmur, but when I finally did, it became routine."

Kemper taught pediatric residents how to sense auras. She told me that she can sense drug withdrawals, prenatal exposure to cocaine, ear infections, and a whole range of other health problems simply by using these techniques.

It would be easy to write off auras as being new-age fluff if science itself hadn't already ridden to the rescue. The existence of an aura around living things has been documented by a number of researchers in a number of ways.

Auras have been seen at UCLA by Dr. Valerie Hunt, a professor emeritus of physics. Using special instruments, she has measured the electromagnetic aura surrounding the human body and has found that it changes in intensity with variations in our health.

These have been captured on X-ray film by a Swedish radiologist named Bjorn Nordenstrom. Because they resemble the corona of the sun, Nordenstrom calls them corona structures. His research shows that these electrical fields exist throughout the body.

Nordenstrom, a well-respected radiologist, feels that this electrical field explains many medical mysteries, including cases where cancers are spontaneously healed.

Dr. Robert Becker, an orthopedic surgeon and professor of medicine at Syracuse University, in New York, sees this force field as a by-product of the electrochemical process that takes place in our body all the time. He has learned to use electromagnetic forces to speed the healing of bones. In one sense he is altering the aura to speed the healing process.

Other doctors have used this electromagnetic force to cure addictions and phobias. Dr. Margaret Patterson, in Great Britain, for example, administers a very light electrical current to the temporal lobes of drug addicts. She has used this technique for almost twenty years and has a very high cure rate.

Dr. Roger Callahan, of Palm Springs, California, uses techniques that resemble acupressure to realign the body's electromagnetic force field. He claims a 90 percent cure rate for his phobic patients, and an 80 percent cure rate for overeaters.

There can be no doubt that we are surrounded by an electromagnetic cloud and that this cloud changes in intensity and perhaps even color with our bodily activity. Valerie Hunt, the researcher at UCLA, even goes so far as to predict that the measurement of auras will become a routine medical procedure as soon as the cost of the instruments comes down.

Once again we have examples of the spiritual world meeting its scientific counterpart. All of a sudden it doesn't seem so foolish to be talking about such things as auras.

Kemper's experience shows how a left-brained skeptic can learn to use her right brain and incorporate it into her daily life. By her own account she is now a better physician, if only because she deals with patients on a holistic basis.

TALENTS WAITING TO BE USED

There are many ways to utilize the spiritual portions of our brain. We don't have to go to Tibet to learn how to do it, or even to be near death. These are ways to tap into our spiritual self, but not the only ways.

Much of our spiritual perception is based on an acceptance of the possibility of a spiritual world in the first place. That doesn't mean we should be gullible. But it does mean that we should be open. Spiritual visions of any sort require thoughtful consideration. They are difficult to understand without it.

Death-related visions can be extra hard to comprehend because of the emotionally charged environment in which they take place.

I think visions are also difficult to interpret because they are mediated through the right temporal lobe. This is the emotional and nonverbal side of our brain. Time is not expressed well on this side of the brain. Neither is precise verbal and rational information. The result can be a powerful spiritual experience that is hard to comprehend and virtually impossible to talk about. When this happens, the experience becomes difficult for the beholder to believe.

I was once speaking to a woman about near-death experiences when she suddenly said, "I wish I could see my father again."

She told me that her father had died when she was thirteen. At that point in her life she had been a mean-spirited adolescent who had lost her appreciation for her father, the most important person in her life. Now she longed to tell him that she was still his little girl and ached to talk to him just one more time.

Even though I didn't know this woman, it was my guess that she had already seen her late father. Parting visions are so common that it is rare for someone to lose a parent or child and not see them again in some kind of death-related vision. The problem is that these experiences are usually overlooked, trivialized, or dismissed out of skepticism. Still they are remembered.

I mentioned the possibility that this may have happened, and she began to nod slowly.

"Well, you might think I am crazy, but he did visit me again," she said. "When I was sixteen, I was driving around with my friends and I crashed the car. We went off the road and into a lake. The car flipped over and began to fill up with water. I was strapped upside down in my seat by the seatbelt. I was terrified.

"Suddenly I felt my dad hugging me. I thought I heard him whisper that everything would be all right. It wasn't a normal hug. It was like I was totally surrounded by him. It stayed that way until we were rescued."

Like so many others, this woman had been able to tap into her own spiritual side when she needed it. Now all she had to do was believe what it told her.

VISIONS AND HEALTH CARE COSTS

It may seem a stretch to relate health care costs to death-related visions. Don't these visions come at the end of a person's life? you might ask. Isn't health care over at that point? The answer to both of those questions is "Sometimes."

Dying people do indeed have visions at the end of their lives, but sometimes these visions take place well before a person's time of death. When they do, they usually provide great comfort to the person from that point on. One of my colleagues calls such visions "morphine for the soul."

But in regard to the other question—when should health care end?—it is no secret that as much as 30 to 60 percent of our health care dollar is spent in the last few days of a person's life. The dirty little secret is that most of it is spent in irrational procedures that do nothing significant to prolong life. In short we are doing all we can do, not all that we should do.

Listening to death-related visions has the potential to dramatically reduce wasteful medical procedures that are often painful to the patient. These procedures are often used on dying patients without their consent and without any hope of prolonging life. The purpose of much of this last-minute medicine is only to make us doctors feel as though everything possible has been done to prevent death, even when death is imminent. The result, writes Dr. William Knaus, of George Washington University, is "to give treatment of no benefit and tremendous cost, depriving others of treatment while dignity disappears."

There is quite a bit of professional debate about the issue of when to stop treatment. Strong families are less likely than weak ones to allow unnecessary treatment to take place. However, it seems as though most people are unwilling to accept the limitations of medical technology. They often threaten lawsuits if everything possible isn't done, even if it makes little sense. Sometimes such an environment forces a physician to overtreat a patient.

Our society has an exaggerated view of what medical technology can accomplish, which is reflected in its desire to completely control the process of dying.

On the surface it may seem hard to see a connection between death-related visions and the overuse of medical technology. But if you think about it, the neglect of spiritual visions by all of those around the deathbed mirrors a great fear of discussing any of the difficult issues surrounding death and dying.

I am not advocating euthanasia or physician-assisted suicide, both of which I am adamantly opposed to. I am not suggesting that we impose religious beliefs upon patients or make them think that they have to have a death-related vision to die a good death. By the same token, medical treatment should not be an either-or situation, where we either commit to "full-bore treatment" or "pull the plug." These situations should be decided on an individual basis.

Research has also shown that paying attention to spiritual issues has an immediate practical effect on human suffering. Paying attention to a patient's feelings and spiritual beliefs can lead to shorter hospital stays and the use of less pain medication. It has also been documented to reduce costs and unnecessary procedures.

Our society denies death. Yet the spiritual aspects of death are clearly no longer taboo. By openly discussing death-related visions we may be able to confront our fear of death and then address the important medical and social issues that go with it. These visions have the power to act as cultural icebreakers.

BREAKING ICE TOWARD A NEW DIALOGUE

I used to think that there was little interest in the subject of death. Even though we all know we are going to die, I sided with Freud when he said, "When we attempt to imagine death, we perceive of ourselves as spectators." I thought there was a tremendous amount of denial and little curiosity about death-related visions.

I have to admit that I myself had little spiritual interest in death-related visions when I first started examining them. I started my research thinking that it would be good for a paper or two.

Not being particularly spiritual or interested in spiritual matters, I thought that my research would show how memory can be utilized in a dying or comatose brain. Understanding how such a coherent memory could come from a brain in distress would amount to a major advance in the field of consciousness research. I believed that at the least near-death experiences would be shown to be a dissociative reaction to drugs, probably one of the dozens of anesthetic agents used during surgery.

I assumed that this research would only be interesting to my peers. I was wrong.

I found that there was intense interest in death-related visions. People from around the world have called or visited to talk about what my research has meant to them. This includes anesthesiologists, psychiatrists, computer experts, mystics, religious fanatics, and ordinary people—all of whom have gone out of their way to discuss death-related visions.

I came to realize that these dramatic visions were just the tip of the iceberg when it came to people's spiritual needs. There were a wide variety of issues related to death and dying that were festering in the collective unconscious.

My first studies, which dealt with the near-death experiences of children, seemed to open the floodgates that held these issues back. My colleagues would call me at night and talk about critically ill patients. Mothers and fathers whose children were dying or had died also called to talk about their loss. A multitude of issues came up in these discussions, usually in the form of questions.

"How can visions be used as healing tools?"

"Why are dying people hooked up to machines that beep? Can't they die just as well without them?"

"Why not help people die who are dying of horrible and incurable diseases?"

"Why isn't death discussed openly so that people who are dying can have a choice between dying in a hospital on a ventilator or dying quietly at home?"

"Why aren't we honest about the costs of dying? Toward the end it makes little sense to spend thousands of dollars to get just a few extra hours of life."

"Why not do everything that *should* be done instead of everything that *can* be done?"

In a very short period of time it was clear to me that people were deeply concerned about spirituality and the issues surrounding it; they just didn't know how to bring it up. The spiritual experiences of innocent children created a context in which death and dying could be openly discussed.

DAILY MIRACLES

I had originally thought that death-related visions were just a reaction to drugs or an undiscovered means of processing memory. I now see them as agents for change, in both society and individuals.

They have certainly changed me. I have gone from being a

cynic about such experiences to becoming a student of their messages. There certainly are many of them.

In many ways my own transformation parallels that of a journalist I met in Europe. I have never met a more cynical and skeptical journalist, which is certainly taking those two traits a long way in light of his profession. He dismissed my work as being nothing more than proof that "children can be as deluded as adults" by the fear of death. Still he was a delightful companion. He had done many stories on the paranormal and occult and had found more fraud than fact in the field. As a result he had concluded that there was no God, only cruel and indifferent nature.

"The only reason I wanted to talk to you is that you think there is an area of the brain that is responsible for generating near-death experiences," he said. "Because of that I think they might be real."

Fine by me, I thought. As we ate, I reviewed the medical literature. We discussed research showing that humans have a large area of their brain devoted to spiritual and mystical abilities. I then emphasized my belief that all death-related visions are paranormal events that happen to normal people.

"It would be good to find such true paranormal events," he said cynically. He then went on to tell me of psychics he had investigated, along with channelers and spiritualists who made money by bilking desperate and lonely people who wanted nothing more than just a few more minutes together with a dead loved one. "It is good to find paranormal events that are real."

Behind the rather thick veneer of cynicism I detected a deep sadness in this journalist. He was like people I met who are looking for something that they haven't yet found, I thought. It was as though he was searching for God in the wrong places and finding man's worst nature instead. I decided to ask him a question.

"How about you?" I probed. "Have you ever had any kind of metaphysical experience?"

He took a sip of wine and acted as though he had not heard my question. Then he asked me something odd.

"Tell me something as a physician," he finally said. "You have seen many people die. Does the body die before the head?"

I told him that generally speaking that was true. First the body dies and then the brain follows a few minutes later, when the oxygenated blood is no longer circulating.

"And what about after death?" he asked. "Does the body cool before the head?"

I was baffled by this line of questioning, but felt that it might be leading somewhere. The journalist seemed to be terribly nervous.

"Everything loses heat at roughly the same rate," I said. "Once the heart stops, everything cools at once."

"I just wondered," he said. "I once felt someone's head who had died and it was very warm and it stayed that way while the rest of the body cooled."

We sat in silence for some time. This had been a strange conversation, and I decided to wait for a few minutes to see if he volunteered any information. Finally he spoke.

"It was my father's head," he said. "His head was very warm more than four hours after his death. My brother and I were there and we both saw it. We thought it was a natural physiological process. My father was no saint, so there would be no reason for something extraordinary to happen."

How do you see a hot head? I wondered.

Finally he told me the whole story. It went like this: He had been estranged from his father and brother for several years, due to some kind of arguments that he didn't elaborate on. When he finally did talk to his brother, it was only to hear the news that their father was dying.

The brothers spent a week together at the bedside of their dying father. The three spoke to each other at length, which they had not done for several years. They realized that the arguments that had torn the family apart were trivial and petty things that should have been put behind them.

"The scene at my father's deathbed was the most loving one my father and I have ever had," said the journalist. "I am sorry that it had to come at the end."

When the father died, the brothers embraced and cried. There had been a death in the family but a healing as well. They knew that through their father's death they would become closer than ever before. It was a strange thing to feel so much personal gain at a time of such great personal loss.

They sat with the body for several hours and talked about many things. It wasn't until almost four hours had passed that they noticed how warm the father's head still felt.

"That was strange," said the journalist. "Because he really had not been this hot in his last days. Isn't it strange that he would be so hot four hours after death?"

The journalist became unusually quiet, so much so that I suspected I had not yet heard the entire story. In my practice I knew that patients will frequently save the most important information for last, often blurting out symptoms or other details as they are leaving the examining room. So it was with this journalist. As our lunch ended and we rose to leave, he rapidly told me the rest of the story.

"But it wasn't that it was just hot," he said, taking me by the elbow as we stood on the sidewalk. "It actually glowed! My brother and I both saw it. Our father's head glowed!"

I knew he was telling me the truth, one so powerful and important that he had kept it hidden all these years. He felt that his father had somehow witnessed the reunion of his sons, and the halo was a reflection of the love he felt.

As we parted, I could see the wonder in his eyes at what he had just told me. I realized that he would continue to investigate the paranormal, seeking to expose frauds. That was good, but would he ignore the miracle of love that had happened right before his very eyes? I hoped not. We have only to trust our own intuitions and feelings, to believe our own perceptions to know that spiritual miracles happen.

Of course there are con men and charlatans who prey on the innocent to enrich themselves. A generation of skeptics have debunked and demystified them. Yet in doing so they have thrown out the baby with the bathwater and have been too cynical to recognize spiritual events that take place right before their eyes. In doing so they ignore an important message, one stated so well earlier in this book by Dr. Frank Oski, of Johns Hopkins University: "I do not ask that others believe what happened to me, I only ask that they keep an open mind to the miracles we witness on a daily basis."

7
VISIONS
IN PRACTICE

—

God is present, like it or not.

—Carl Jung

A touching story of a man's final hours was told to me by Dr. Charles Lewis, a physician who works with the dying at San Diego Hospice.

The man was dying of AIDS and asked Lewis what he could expect as he died. Lewis told the man that many people who have had near-death experiences describe going into a bright light. He did not tell him about the other possibilities, such as traveling up a tunnel or meeting a being of light.

The man's death was unusual in that he was entirely conscious during the dying process. As the hospice staff and the man's family listened in awe, he began to describe what he saw as he left this world. His eyes opened wide and he began to smile. A bright light had entered the room, he said to the people gathered around the bed.

"Please move back," he said, looking straight ahead as the light that only he could see grew in size and intensity.

No one present was surprised that he saw such a light, since Lewis had prepared him for just such an event. Then the man began talking about things Lewis had never mentioned. He told them that he could see a tunnel with a man "inside of light" who was standing next to a gate. The gate was opening and he was going through it, he said. Then he died.

This is an excellent example of everyone pulling together to actually listen to the needs of the patient. There was no chaos at the bedside with futile efforts to try to save him. There was no cynicism as the patient described the visions, just as there was no effort to pull him back from the brink of death and ignore what he was seeing. Quite simply everyone just listened and allowed the visions to ease the death.

Years of medical school and related training have taught doctors to listen to complaints about sore throats, dizziness, and other physical symptoms. Spiritual crisis, however, brings on a host of psychological dilemmas that physicians are ill prepared to handle. When it comes to death and death-related visions, physicians are usually no better at handling the stress and emotions of watching a person die than is the average family member. As a result such crises are usually mishandled.

A nurse at a Cleveland hospital gave me an excellent example of how hard it is for some doctors to relate to patients in spiritual crisis. She told me of a patient who came into the emergency room complaining of severe chest pains that felt like an elephant was sitting on his chest. The man soon turned blue and went into a full cardiac arrest. The cardiologist on the scene, a physician in his sixties, began lifesaving measures, and the patient's heartbeat was soon restored.

Late that evening the man talked to this same doctor in the intensive care unit. They talked about his condition and the measures that had been taken to save the man's life. He thanked the doctor profusely. Then he asked a question, which the nurse heard as she stood there behind the doctor.

"Where did I go when all of this stuff was going on?"

"What do you mean?" asked the doctor.

"I felt like I went into this tunnel at about a hundred miles an hour and I came out in a beautiful place, sort of like a forest of light. I think I saw things out of my life from when I was a young man. Then I came back. What was that all about?"

The nurse said that the doctor seemed unprepared for the question. He could handle questions about resuscitation and heart monitors, but he wasn't ready for any conversation that drifted into the metaphysical.

"So, what was it, doc?" demanded the patient. "Does that kind of thing happen to any other patients?"

"Not if I can help it," he said, beating a hasty retreat from the room.

The nurse laughed when she told me the story, and I have to admit that I laughed, too, but the humor had an edge to it. For all of his technical expertise this physician was simply not prepared to handle a spiritual crisis. By relying on information in the same medical journals that made him an efficient technician, he could have alleviated some of his patient's stress over his illness. He also could have lessened his own stress, especially for the times when he was not fortunate enough to bring a patient back to life.

By relying on the medical research done in just the last ten years, he could have delivered a healing message to his patient without feeling less of a scientist. Here is what he could have told this man:

■ *"There is simply no reason to think you are crazy."* There is no research linking these experiences to pathology or dysfunction. Also there is no reason to consider them hallucinations, which are roundly considered to be negative by the medical community. Death-related visions are usually positive and lack such factors as paranoia, negative imagery, distortions of reality, and aggressive and hostile actions—all of which are associated with psychotic behavior. They occur to people who are in excellent mental health and are in no way associated with mental illness.

- *"You didn't make up this experience."* Some people are told that they "made up" the spiritual experience as a way of avoiding reality. But the scientific evidence says that death-related visions are not made up later, but take place when a person says they do. This means that they happen in "real time" and are as real as any other human experience.

- *"Your spiritual experience will most likely change you for the better."* One of the hallmarks of death-related visions is that they cause long-lasting changes in personality. From a single brief experience, controlled studies have shown a decrease in neurotic anxiety, a perception of life having meaning and purpose, an increased sense of one's spiritual life, a belief in an afterlife, and even a healing of addictions. Carefully conducted studies have shown that people who have near-death experiences, for example, use fewer over-the-counter drugs, eat more fresh vegetables, give more money to charity, and do more physical exercise than those who haven't had them. These studies document that spiritual experiences profoundly affect a person's life in ways that wish-fulfilling fantasies and dreams do not.

- *"These experiences are empowering for the dying."* Death-related visions improve the quality of death as well as the quality of life. For the dying patient it is a relief to know that the dying process will not be painful and may contain visits with departed loved ones. For the survivors these experiences create new and healthier meanings of life and death. It is important for surviving family members to note that pre-death visions and post-death visitations can be strikingly similar to near-death experiences. They frequently contain such elements as the presence of spiritual beings, visions of a loving and spiritual light, and the sudden appearance of departed loved ones.

These visions have even been shared by living family members and friends. For example a nurse wrote in a medical journal of a vision that occurred to her when a patient close to her died. She reported rising out of her physical body and traveling with the patient into a spiritual light.

Post-death visitations happen more often than not. More than fifty years of medical studies show that a majority of widows as well as parents who have lost children have visions of the departed within a year of their death. Although some of these studies refer to these visions as hallucinations, they are in fact positive experiences that help heal the grief.

SCIENCE WITHOUT GUILT

Without becoming less of a scientist this man's physician could have become more of a healer. All of this is hard-core science, not philosophy or religion or speculation. All he had to do was rely on scientific studies published in the medical journals that form the bedrock information that medicine is built on.

Yet the medical establishment pays little attention to these vitally important spiritual events. By doing so they miss a chance for healing that even they themselves could benefit from. After all, no one in our society deals more with death than the medical doctor. As the noted psychologist Stanislav Grof has commented, "In connection with our success- and efficiency-oriented philosophy, aging and dying are not integrated parts of life, but a defeat and a painful reminder of our limits in controlling nature. . . . Fighting for the mechanical prolongation of life, the quality of the patient's last days and his psychic and spiritual longings do not receive enough attention."

If my research has taught me anything, it is that death-related visions need to be accorded the same respect and dignity that we extend to mothers with colicky infants or middle-aged men going through midlife crisis. At their very least death-related visions are a developmental stage of life that come with loss and death.

"WHERE IS THAT LIGHT COMING FROM?"

A woman I'll call Janice provides an excellent example of what I am talking about. When she was nineteen, her father had a stroke and died two weeks later. His death was a terrifying experience that haunted her for years to come. She developed an almost pathological fear of death and of old people. She was also terrified of losing another family member.

Nine years later her mother became fatally ill with small-cell lung cancer. Shortly before the diagnosis Janice became interested in death-related visions. She read several books on the subject, including *Closer to the Light*, which I wrote in 1989.

"Just knowing about these experiences gave me a different perspective on death," she told me.

No longer frightened of at least discussing death, she shared her knowledge of the dying experience with her mother, who was then in the hospice wing at the hospital. Janice found that she now viewed death differently and was able to spend time around those who were dying without the fear she had felt when her father was dying. So she was able to spend much more time with her mother during her final hours than any of the other family members. Where other family members expressed guilt at not having the emotional strength to spend time in the hospice wing, Janice devoted herself to caring for her mother in her final days. As a result she had none of the guilt often expressed by family members who feel they should be at the bedside but cannot deal with the emotions of death.

One evening when most of the family sat in the room, the mother awoke and said, "Where is that light coming from? It is so bright."

"My family members were closing curtains and flicking light switches," she said. "But I knew exactly what light my mother was talking about. She was going to the spiritual light." A few days later her mother died.

Shortly after her mother passed away, Janice had a very moving death-related vision of her own. She was sitting at home in the dark when she heard a voice say clearly, "Would you be afraid to see her again in the light?"

She suddenly realized that this meant that she would see her mother again when she herself died and entered into that same light. This experience signaled the end of her grief.

These experiences would be easy to trivialize, as many people did after she told them what had happened, but for Janice they were transformative experiences. She began to work with the terminally ill in a local hospice. It is not uncommon now for her to share her experiences with dying people. Janice is proof that death-related visions empower the living as well as the dying.

Frankly I find it hard to be skeptical in the face of stories like this one. I find it hard to belittle and trivialize these experiences when their healing possibilities are so powerful and obvious that they deserve only validation and respect.

NOT PREPARED TO LISTEN

The problem with much of the medical establishment today is that it is not trained to listen, nor is it encouraged to do so. Our medical institutions, hospitals, insurance companies, and even our system of grant distribution at the federal level are based upon a set of beliefs that largely deny that the human spirit has anything to do with health or the functioning of the biological machine.

For example, several studies have documented that surgery patients go home sooner if an anesthesiologist takes a few minutes to explain postoperative pain. Few anesthesiologists do such counseling on their own since most insurance companies don't pay them to do so. They are certainly aware of these studies, but regard them as irrelevant phenomena, something not related to the "real" medicine of administering medications and doing procedures.

Although most people consider themselves to be spiritual beings, our intellectual and scientific leaders deny that humankind's spiritual side is all that important. They describe

events such as death-related visions as being "just psychological." This terminology is embedded in our medical jargon,
and every physician knows that. *Psychosocial in origin, functional pain,* and *nonorganic in etiology* are phrases that are in-
terchangeable with *just psychological.* They signal that the
doctor should stop thinking about the case and get on with
other patients, that this patient has a psychological problem.
Insurance companies know what those words mean as well,
and they will not pay for hospitalization or doctor visits with
those sorts of diagnosis.

Still, pain that is "nonorganic in etiology" does not make a
statement about the cause of pain so much as it assumes that
we understand everything about the body and everything that
could cause various conditions. Medical journals are filled
with disease processes that do not fit neatly into diagnostic categories. The sad reality is that by focusing on a relatively few
easy-to-treat diagnoses, we have dramatically limited the scope
of modern medicine. All of this reminds me of what one of my
professors at Johns Hopkins said: "Mel, most doctors get
through medical school and think they are God because they
know a little about the human body. The really good ones are
humbled by how much they don't know."

OUR UNDERVALUED SPIRIT

Our working models of science and society permit very little
understanding of man as a spiritual being. Claims adjusters at
insurance companies don't consciously try to ignore the spiritual side of medicine, they are just blind to it. As a result they
pay doctors to do medical procedures, while any counseling

and education we do is paid for out of our own pockets. Even though we might know that a patient's complaint is "just psychological," we still have to do tests and procedures in order to make everybody happy. This is our technological ritual, one that devalues our spiritual side.

This is not just a medical problem.

The split between religion and science took place hundreds of years ago, when Galileo angered the Catholic church by discovering the nature of the solar system, but the rift has become even wider in the last fifty years. Now society lacks the spiritual "glue" that holds us together and explains the meaning of life. Problems such as alcoholism, drug addiction, and depression all represent a failure of the human spirit, a lack of conviction by individuals that their lives are important. Let's face it, the message of hope and meaning that comes from death-related visions and other visionary experiences is a major reason that my books and others like them have been so popular. The messages contained in them fill a spiritual void and add meaning to one's life.

Which brings us back to where we began, the need for all of us to attend to the spiritual needs of the dying.

The bond between physician and patient can unravel as death approaches or when death-related visions are brought into the discussion. Death can make a doctor feel like a failure, a feeling that is often promoted by patients who expect too much from medicine. In our current climate of nonacceptance visions make everyone—the people who have them as well as those who hear about them—feel uncomfortable.

A GUIDE TO UNDERSTANDING

As I proceeded with my research, I realized that death and the puzzling experiences that surround it are hard for both patient and doctor to cope with. There was a need for guidelines to show people how to find their way. I spent days wading through my own research and records, from data and case studies to letters and phone calls. Gradually a therapeutic framework began to emerge for those in spiritual crisis. I published a version of these guidelines in *Current Problems in Pediatrics*, under the title "Death-Related Visions: Theoretical Implications for Clinical Practice." I am not saying that these are comprehensive guidelines. But at least they are a beginning, something that can lead to further discussion.

Those Having Death-Related Visions May Require Counseling. Whether the death-related vision is a near-death experience, a pre-death vision, or a post-death visitation, it will certainly precipitate a state of spiritual emergency. People who have these experiences have difficulty understanding what has happened to them. At its worst the experience can be frightening; at its best it can be wonderful. Either way emotional adjustment will take place as the patient is forced to reassess his life and goals.

In ten years of counseling patients who have had these experiences, I have encountered the following sorts of questions:

■ If near-death experiences involve a choice to "stay" or "return to life," does it follow that children who die choose not to return?

■ If a child is in a prolonged coma, does that mean he or she is "stuck in the tunnel" or somehow unable to complete the death experience?

■ Why do some people have hellish or negative experiences? What about those who only experience a dark void or don't have any spiritual experience at all?

■ Why do some family members have death-related visitations and others don't? For many families death-related visions can lead to further family chaos as different value judgments and spiritual interpretations are placed on the experience.

As belief and understanding of death-related visions become more common, such questions will increasingly be broached to caregivers.

Death-Related Visions Can Lessen Grief. Mourning involves four distinct stages: grieving, accepting the loss, reattaching to the community, and reinvesting emotional energy. Death-related visions can help at each of these stages if they are used therapeutically to affirm spiritual intuitions and faith.

It is important to realize that death-related visions are sometimes vague. Some of these experiences involve only a faint smile at the point of death or a brief comment such as "The light, the light," or "I am on a rocketship to the moon."

Premonitions of death often involve only vague perceptions or feelings, which nonetheless can establish faith that life and death have meaning.

Post-death visitations often involve contact with the dead, which allows the loss to be accepted so that the person can then reinvest his or her emotional energy.

In my role as counselor at these times I have found that it is usually best to listen and to let the person put his or her own meaning on the experience. Spiritual counseling is difficult.

People often lash out in unpredictable ways when dealing with the emotional issues surrounding death and dying.

It is important to keep in mind that no one is always good at talking to people at a time of loss. The task is frequently thankless and the results are not immediately visible. I have said what I thought was the right thing only to have family members lash out at me. Still I realize that even these emotions are healthy because they have opened the door to an area of themselves that most people keep closed.

These Visions Can Restore Dignity to the Process of Dying. Dying can be a dehumanizing and spiritually degrading process. Patients often die alone, stripped of personal dignity. They feel that they are useless and a burden to their families, often draining financial resources for expensive care that is of little benefit.

Just knowing about death-related visions can change this. Family members who know about the visions of the dying are known to spend more time at the dying person's bedside. This factor alone alleviates much of the guilt they might feel after the loved one's death.

Spiritual visions can empower dying patients as well. For one thing they realize that they still have something important to share with others. For another just hearing the reports of others who have almost died gives them courage in knowing that the dying process is not a painful one.

As a caregiver it is important to know that even the sadness of death can be life-affirming and healing when it takes place within a spiritual context.

These Visions Can Prevent Burnout. To be an effective caregiver, you need to take care of your own emotional needs as well. Health care professionals often erect emotional barriers and resort to irrational routines and procedures designed as protection against the pain of the impending deaths of their patients.

The brutality of modern medicine coupled with the use of painful and invasive procedures for dying patients has a way of dehumanizing those around the deathbed, which results in spiritual despair and emotional burnout.

This is true of family members as well. Although they are not ministering to their loved one in the same way that the doctors and nurses are, they usually demand additional procedures even in the face of a futile situation.

Death-related visions of all kinds have the potential to change our approach to dying patients while supplying us with spiritual nourishment at a time of great need.

I have a story that illustrates how a dying patient's vision provided a spiritual bolstering for a caregiver. This happened to a medical doctor in California, who had been caring for a child with cancer for several years and was now making house calls to visit his patient as he lay dying.

These were the boy's last few days, and they were stressful ones for everyone. The doctor had taken a special liking to this boy and had pursued every treatment possible. Now that all of them had failed, there was nothing for him to do except join the family at his bedside and make his final hours as comfortable as possible.

On the last day of this child's life maintaining composure was difficult for everyone. As is true at the deathbed of most children, there was a lot of anger and frustration at the horrible hand each of these onlookers had been dealt by fate. As the boy began to die, the agony in the room became overwhelming.

Suddenly the boy opened his eyes and looked at a spot in the room where no one was standing. "Grandpa," he said. "Hi, Grandpa!"

Immediately the mother hugged the boy. It was her father who had died two years earlier that the boy saw. Now the mother seemed to be revived by her son's vision. They spoke for a few seconds about what he saw, and then the mother said, "Go to Dad now, he's waiting for you."

This brief yet vivid vision gave the family a handle on their grief. Losing their son was not easy, but knowing that he was being greeted by his grandfather made it easier for them to bear.

Witnessing this experience also made the pain of losing a patient easier for the doctor. As he told me, "I had done everything I could. Now I could see that it was time for forces greater than medicine to take over."

These Are Not Just "Warm Fuzzy" Ways to Die. Most valuable of all is the realization that death-related visions are a natural response to death, not pathological hallucinations or fantasies.

The acceptance by the medical establishment of the existence or validity of death-related visions has the potential to reduce wasteful and irrational medical procedures and treatments dramatically. Almost 30 percent of our health care dollars are spent in the last few months of life in a vain attempt to keep patients alive longer. It is my opinion that expensive and dehumanizing medical procedures are often used on dying patients without their consent and without any hope of prolonging life. We use these procedures to make ourselves feel that we did everything possible to prevent death.

Personally I have treated many dying patients and found myself ordering unnecessary lab tests simply to assure myself that I had done everything I could to prolong life. I know from talking to other health care workers that my experience is not unique.

Research shows that we rely too much on expensive medical tests, which are easy to document and justify yet that lead to nothing more than a higher hospital bill. Dr. Susan Bratton, a pediatric intensivist at Seattle Children's Hospital, feels that dying children are often overtreated with intensive-care-unit technology.

Patients often receive such treatments as a matter of routine, she says. There is also a darker side to the use of medical technology. Doctors fear litigation from parents who want "everything possible" to be done without realizing that these desperate procedures are painful and will add very little to the prolongation of life.

Cardiopulmonary resuscitation, for example, is described as being "experimental in nature" with little chance of benefit. Yet it is used on a vast majority of dying patients. On the other hand, paying attention to spiritual issues can lead to significantly shorter hospital stays and even to a decreased use of pain medication.

I am not advocating euthanasia or physician-assisted suicide. Rather I am just stating the facts about the economic and health value of these visions.

Even if we are attuned to them, death-related visions might be difficult to understand. Still we should honor the patient by listening to him and validating his feelings and intuitions. That doesn't mean that we try to play the role of chaplain or social worker. All it means is that we need to keep an open mind in dealing with paranormal events that surround death and dying. Regardless of their cause, these experiences have the power to heal.

Death-Related Visions Let Us Live More Fully. "Death is the worm at the core of our happiness," said Sigmund Freud. That is certainly true for people who have not explored the subject of death-related visions. For those who have, or for those who have actually *had* one, the gnawing of that worm is greatly diminished.

My own research has shown that death anxiety is much lower in people who have had near-death experiences or mystical experiences. The study conducted by Vernon Larson showed a decreased death anxiety in people who have even only read about near-death experiences.

Clearly there is comfort in both having a death-related vision and knowing about them, a comfort that allows people to live life to its fullest. There are many excellent examples of people losing their fear of death after having a death-related vision. But perhaps the best example is a story about Dannion Brinkley, which comes from my coauthor, Paul Perry.

The two were in Tampa, Florida, working on the best-selling book *Saved by the Light*, an account of the near-death experience Brinkley had after being struck by lightning in 1975. Much of Brinkley's heart was destroyed by the lightning, a fact that makes it dangerous for him to exert himself.

The two were walking fast when Brinkley began to breathe heavily and to complain of chest pains. By the time they got off their feet in a fast-food restaurant, Brinkley had begun to turn blue and to gasp for air.

There was general panic. Patrons gathered around to offer advice, and the people behind the counter wanted to call the emergency medical team, which Perry also wanted them to do.

The only person in the room who was not afraid was Brinkley himself. Through the pain and lack of oxygen he laughed at the thought of an ambulance showing up.

"Just forget the doctors," he said. "I've died before and I liked it."

It is examples such as this one, people who are on the brink of death yet exhibit no fear, that show the ability of these visions to quell death anxiety.

CHANGING THE MEANING OF CONTROL

As I circulated the message in my paper on death-related visions, I was greeted with a number of interesting responses. A medical student wrote me a note that said, "Perhaps if people understood that it is not so scary to die, our society would find new rituals to interpret death and dying and our society would heal itself in the process."

I delivered a talk to a group of intensive-care-unit nurses during which I told them many of the stories contained in this book and then offered the guidelines that I presented in the paper. When I finished my talk, these battle-hardened nurses stood up and cheered. One by one they told me stories of how they had become burned out by dealing unrealistically with death. One of them wept as she said, "I didn't want to come to this lecture, I thought you would be too sappy. Now that I have heard you speak, I recognize that I have let something in myself die. I have lost something in my own spirituality that helps me be myself and helps me deal honestly with my patients."

The comment that truly hit home for me came from an emergency room physician, who told me about the helplessness he so often feels when people are brought in on the brink of death. Cardiac arrest, gunshot wounds, motorcycle accidents—this physician had seen it all. Although he had become very proficient at the technical aspects of preventing death, the defeated feelings he had when he failed were overwhelming. Sometimes he couldn't sleep because he felt he had "failed" to stop death. "I was angry because I couldn't control it," he said. As a result of my lecture he realized that death is a part of the fabric of life. As he put it, "For me this research changes the definition of control."

OBVIOUSLY NOT IN CONTROL

I knew exactly what he meant. As a medical resident I studied hard to become the best that I could be at emergency medicine. This meant becoming an expert at cardiopulmonary resuscitation and at performing lifesaving surgical procedures. It meant putting a barrier between myself and the terrible things I was seeing. It meant being fast, efficient, decisive, and in control.

It also meant pretending to be in control even when we obviously were not.

One such case happened while I was a physician for Air Northwest, an emergency airlift service based in Seattle. One time we flew to a remote area to pick up a child who had drowned in an open septic tank. The child had been submerged for seventy-five minutes and had no chance of living. By the time we arrived, he had been laid out next to the tank by the members of the volunteer fire department that had pulled him from the muck. His father stood hopelessly beside him and watched as we charged out of the helicopter.

The child had no heartbeat. I filled a syringe with a drug designed to "flog" the heart into action and stuck it into his chest. I began putting the boy on a breathing machine as everyone watched in stunned silence.

"Why are we doing this?" asked one of the nurses.

I ignored her.

"Excuse me, doctor," said the boy's father. "Is this necessary?"

I ignored the courage that it took for him to ask that question. "Of course," I said. "We'll do everything we can to save your son's life."

I was ignoring the fact that his son was alive in heartbeat only. Four days later and hundreds of miles from home, the boy died in an intensive care unit.

It was only then that I questioned the rationale for what I had done. The boy was dead when we got there, I realized. I only created the illusion that he was alive. I could resuscitate the body but not the brain. If I had faced the reality of the situation, the family would have been spared the agony of false hope.

"I WAS UP THERE AND
COULD SEE EVERYTHING"

I have had many discussions about life and death with nurses and have heard many parting visions in return. For example one nurse recalled an event that took place during her student years in South Dakota. It was her first day in intensive care. She and a nurse were caring for an old rancher with heart disease.

They were standing around his bed when the rancher suddenly had a heart attack and flatlined. They brought over a cardioversion machine and did the best they could to hook it up. In their haste and inexperience the paddles were put on backward, and the lifesaving machine would not function as it was supposed to. Finally, they reversed the paddles and restarted the man's heart.

Later the next day, the nurse who was telling me this story came back to the man's room for a visit. When she came in, he grinned and wagged his index finger at her. "I know that voice," he said. "I saw you discuss with a nurse which way the paddles would go. I tried to tell you I was okay."

"What do you mean?" she said.

"You thought I was dead." He laughed. "But I was up there and I could see everything. I could see myself and I could see you hooking up the machine wrong."

This story teaches me that we are not in as much control as we like to think we are.

I have heard hundreds of case studies that I wouldn't have heard without the marvels of modern medical technology and the perseverance of doctors and nurses who wanted to try just one more lifesaving measure.

But I have become more accepting of the cycle of life and death. I have learned to forgive myself for those times when my best just wasn't good enough. And I have taken comfort in the knowledge that the dying process contains visions of an intensely spiritual nature that have the power to affect virtually everyone, not only the dying but their loved ones and health care workers alike.

8

THE SIGNIFICANCE OF PARTING VISIONS IN EVERYDAY LIFE

—

Everything that you do in life is insignificant.
Yet it is important that you do it.

—Mahatma Gandhi

My grand conclusion, after twelve years of listening to the near-death experiences of children, is neither grand nor new. I have learned to be open to the many miracles that we encounter in our ordinary lives. I do not expect to see an angel or to have the sort of spiritual experience described in my book until I die. Yet my scientific studies of death-related visions have convinced me that our ordinary lives are filled with purpose and meaning. The importance of near-death studies is not what they teach us about life after death, but rather the spotlight they shine on the spiritual impoverishment of our own lives.

I firmly believe that every person has something of importance to learn from studying the visions that surround the dying process. These experiences teach us that what we do is important and that all of life is interconnected. I am not speaking metaphorically when I make such a statement. The one inescapable conclusion of near-death research is that there is a divine "something," which serves as a glue for the universe. A nuclear physicist might try to describe that glue as an electromagnetic equation; a religious philosopher might call it God.

The evidence for this godly glue is not difficult to find. We have only to examine our own thoughts and feelings and intuitions, and the events of our own lives. Often the best evidence for the truth of my conclusion can be found in seemingly meaningless coincidences and banal inspirations.

I would like to emphasize that I have reached this conclusion from my beginnings as an arrogant critical-care physician. I do not have a religious faith and was raised in a nominally Jewish household. My idea of a good time is to watch a basketball game or play baseball with my boys. I do not own love beads or robes and have a violent allergy to anything remotely "New Age." I am too busy with my practice of medicine, my five children, and our small horse ranch to spend time meditating or raising my consciousness.

I completely understand the profound skepticism about near-death research common to most scientists and physicians. I also have an emotional block against accepting the logical conclusions of near-death research. Recently, I interviewed a young boy who nearly suffocated to death in a collapsed tunnel. He told me that he was fully conscious during the experience and that a wizard dressed in white appeared to him and told him to "struggle and I would live." He said he was surrounded by a white light during the time he was documented to have been clinically dead. After all the hundreds of experiences I have heard about, I was impressed at the simplicity and sincerity of his experience, and I found myself thinking,

"Wow, maybe there is really something in this after all!" Clearly he did not invent this story from watching too many Oprah Winfrey shows. This was the first "wizard" I had encountered in my studies.

Although I have an emotional bias against anything spiritual, intellectually I recognize that near-death research strongly supports the concept of some form of life after death, and that certain aspects of human consciousness must be independent of brain function. The quality of this research is quite low, and is not of sufficient caliber for any firm conclusions to be reached. Nevertheless, it is now scientifically respectable to discuss the survival hypothesis.

Such considerations are ultimately a sideshow, a distraction from the real value and worth of understanding death-related visions. We now know that we do not simply die and go into darkness. Instead there is a loving light awaiting us all when we die. What exists beyond that final light of life is still, of course, unknown. What is far more difficult to understand and accept is that that same light is ever present throughout our lives.

I did not write this book to discuss a light after death. I wrote this book to help people understand that there is a spiritual light in our lives that we all see when we die. This is one aspect of near-death experiences with which everyone agrees, a common ground that skeptic and believer alike share. Since recognizing that spiritual light was the message of the near-death experience, I have validated this concept again and again in my own life as well as in the lives of others. In this final chapter, I would like to present aspects of death-related visions that should not be controversial, and that have the power to change our lives and our society.

NEAR-DEATH EXPERIENCES REPRESENT THE ONLY
OBJECTIVE EVIDENCE OF WHAT IT IS LIKE TO DIE

We will all die. No matter how many heart transplants we
have, or vitamins we take, we still will die. For most of my life I
was unaware of that fact, until I recently turned forty. After witnessing hundreds of deaths of patients and writing two books
on death and dying, it may seem odd that I never really
thought about my own death. Well, I am thinking about it
now. I have become all too aware of my own mortality and it
frightens me.

Throughout the ages and cultures we have all feared death,
and yet little is known about what it is we fear. Ultimately, we
fear the end of life, coupled with anxiety about the unknown.
The Greek philosopher Heraclitus said, "All that we see when
we have awakened is death; all that we see while slumbering is
sleep." This knowledge of the transient and ever changing nature of life is even embedded in our children's songs. I grew up
singing "Row, row, row your boat, gently down the stream,
Merrily, merrily, merrily, merrily, Life is but a dream" without
ever listening to the lyrics and understanding their meaning.

Medical science has shed light on what happens when we
die, in that we now have the ability to resuscitate so many real-
life flatliners. Literally millions of people have survived clinical death. Often I am asked why all of them don't remember
some sort of near-death experience. I respond that given the
medications and clinical interventions they are subjected to, it
is understandable that only a certain percentage retain the
memory of their experience. It is man's technological genius
and rational self that has led to new philosophical understand-
ings of the nature of the human soul.

The fact that my father, who has died, or my wife, if she dies before me, will be present to help me when I die is enormously reassuring. We are comforted in dying by those same images and people who loved us during our lives. Pets, stuffed animals, guardian angels, living teachers, beloved grandparents; they come to help us when we die.

Dying is not always scary or painful. Mountain climbers who fall from great heights and live report that they often hear and see the impact of their bodies but rarely feel it. A young boy who nearly drowned told me that "God took me out [of my body] and kept me safe" during the time he was dying and his ultimate resuscitation. We are usually conscious during our deaths, even when we are perceived to be comatose, and can hear and see events happening in our immediate vicinity.

Clearly, consciousness persists at least many minutes after the cessation of the rest of the functions of the body and brain. Anthropologist Chris Carr, in his crosscultural studies of near-death experiences, concludes that dying is a reality for learning, and offers opportunity for growth. In essence, dying is no different from the rest of living in its essential purposes. Sitting at the bedside of a dying comatose patient is an excellent time to talk and perhaps settle old hurts and differences.

For example, a woman told me of her experience of sitting at the bedside of her husband, who was dying of an unexpected heart attack. He was comatose, and hooked up to life-support machinery. Her shock and grief was made all the more complex in that she had not resolved her anger over his recent disclosure that he was having an affair with a younger woman.

Fortunately for this woman, she had a close friend who had had a near-death experience. Her friend encouraged her to speak to her husband, just as if he were alive. She not only spoke to him, but she found herself ultimately screaming at him, shouting at him, swearing at him. I can only imagine the nurses' reactions to her behavior. I know that it could never have occurred without the support of her friend, who had first-hand knowledge that comatose dying patients often have complete awareness and can process conversations emotionally. Finally her fury was spent, and she cried, and spoke lovingly of the life they had had together. He died soon after this life review.

My rational, skeptical nature considers his abrupt death to be a meaningless coincidence. The woman was simply reading meaning into events while being influenced with irrational expectations that her husband was having a near-death experience. Or perhaps all that shouting and screaming upset him physiologically and precipitated his death. It is possible, however, that the most scientific explanation for this man's death was that he did hear his wife and that they had resolved their unfinished business. An event that seems coincidental on the surface becomes understandable when we review our knowledge of the dying process.

I have heard many reports from clinically dead children I have resuscitated, children with whom I was present during their near-death. These children repeatedly told precise details of their own resuscitations. "I saw you put a tube in my nose." "The tall thin doctor said to you he was glad you were there." "They cut off my clothes with scissors and my hair was all messed up." "There were two lady doctors and they had green masks." "I saw Dr. Herndon put paddles on me and he sucked me back into my body." One boy, Patrick Nicholson, was featured on a 20/20 documentary that demonstrated that he saw precise details of his own dramatic rescue from nearly drowning that were verified by photographs taken of the scene, photographs he had never seen and of which he had no knowledge.

Sometimes people get a dramatic preview of their own death that can change their lives for the better. While we are living, we are storing and developing the events and images that will be present for us when we die. These images and experiences are stored within our right temporal lobes.

The best evidence for this is seen in people who have right-temporal-lobe seizures. A seizure represents the unwanted and uncoordinated electrical activity of an area of the brain. If we have a seizure in our motor cortex, for example, our right hand might meaninglessly move and spasm again and again. A similar event in our right temporal lobe can lead to the elements of the dying experience, including the out-of-body perceptions, the tunnel, and our personal vision of heaven being replayed, often again and again, without meaning.

A patient of mine, Tina Mashore, told me that she had somewhat frightening and puzzling dreams about dying. One dream involved a vivid out-of-body sensation coupled with a knowledge that she was dead. A second involved a perception of vivid consciousness coupled with an absolute knowledge that she was in heaven. While in heaven, she heard her grandmother-in-law calling to her, and knew that she must ignore that call to continue to live.

These are examples of lucid dreams. They occur at a different stage of sleep than ordinary dreams. Near-death experiences are similar to lucid dreams in that the same brain machinery is utilized and both often contain vivid out-of-body perceptions. But they are not like ordinary dreams, which are often associated with processing the events of the day and REM sleep.

I explained to Mrs. Mashore that her dreams did not mean that she was going to die soon, as she erroneously believed. Instead, her dream represented the inadvertent firing of neuronal circuitry, which resulted in a preview for her of what will happen and what she will perceive when she does die. For example, her "heaven" will have white clouds that she will walk through.

As a part of validating my theory for myself, I then said: "And the proof of this is that your grandmother-in-law is clearly your 'guardian angel,' your spiritual helper." She confirmed that this was so. Her "Grannie" was the only person who stuck up for her in a hundred pointless family battles. She felt there was a deep and unspoken bond between her and Grannie. "She was the only one who told me that everything would be okay."

Mrs. Mashore now says these dreams were wonderfully comforting experiences, once she understood their significance. She says that she is not afraid to die.

I learned from these experiences that we die the life we live. I have never interviewed anyone who had a near-death experience who told me that they came back to make more money or to spend more time at their jobs away from their families. Rarely do they tell me that they learned they were not selfish enough or greedy enough. Instead they become convinced that they need to be more loving and kind. They react to their experience by living life to its fullest. They believe their lives have a purpose, even if that purpose is obscure to them. Invariably it involves concepts such as love of family or service to others. They seem to know that the love they create while living will be reflected and radiated back to them when they die.

HELLISH EXPERIENCE, HELLISH LIFE

Now we can understand the significance of the hellish near-death experience. It too is often a reflection of life, but of an unhappy, hellish life. I once interviewed a man who had such an experience. He had been a teenage gangster, a violent man interested only in his own personal gain. He nearly died when he was slashed with a broken bottle while attempting to rob a convenience store. While in the ambulance on the way to the hospital, he perceived himself being pulled out of his body while it burst into flames. Instead of perceiving loving guardian angels, he said that the faces of his friends who had died on the street appeared to him, crying in pain that they said would never end. As a result of his experience, he left his life of crime and ultimately became ordained as a minister.

My own life has been transformed by my research. I try to spend a lot more time with my family. I have taken to heart what one little girl told me she learned from her near-death experience: "It's nice to be nice, Dr. Morse." The knowledge that when we die we perceive another reality that quite literally sheds light on this one somehow motivates me to be a better person. As Seneca once said, "Men do not care how nobly they live, but only how long, although it is within the reach of every man to live nobly, but within no man's power to live long."

The question remains: Is this light and this perception of another reality real? If certain brain structures are devoted to perceiving the experience, does that mean this light originates from outside our body, or is simply generated by neurochemistry? These are the questions to which everyone seems to want to know the answers. It is not enough simply to want to create a better world for the sake of our children or to love one another. A large part of me wants proof that God exists.

It is my firm opinion that such proof will never exist, not the kind of proof for which most people are looking. I have never encountered or heard of a case that provided hard evidence in near-death research. Ideally, such a case would involve an angel leaving behind a heavenly trinket made of a metal that does not exist on Earth and stamped "Made by God." I have stopped expecting or looking for this sort of proof.

I have come to realize that the proof comes in a better understanding of what is reality, not in expecting that the laws of nature will suspend themselves. I am suggesting that through studying near-death experiences we will come to a new understanding of the nature of reality, and thereby better understand the nature of what we call god.

Most people are unaware that we do not directly perceive reality, but rather are constantly creating images of what we think we see, in our brain. Our eyes are not videocameras, and our ears are not microphones. Instead, our eyes, for example, are constantly bombarding our brain with input such as "red or green spot," or "wiggly line that just stopped moving," and we create a visual image from that information, in our occipital lobes. It is accurate to say that we surmise reality, we infer reality. We certainly do not perceive it directly.

When the input from our eyes and ears ceases, as it does during death, our brain relies on other input to create a different reality. Sometimes this other reality intrudes in our dreams, or can be superimposed over our other perceptions in a variety of different situations. There is no reason to suppose that these perceptions are any more or less real than any other perceptions.

The information we obtain from these perceptions of another reality is real and verifiable. People who have visions of this type enjoy excellent mental health and actually live healthier and more productive lives than the rest of us. There is some evidence that they are actually physically changed by their encounter with the light. It may alter the subtle electromagnetic fields that surround our bodies. Numerous studies document the positive transformative effect of having near-death experiences.

It could be argued that vivid hallucinations could have the same effects. I agree that this evidence is circumstantial at best. The value of these studies is to document that near-death experiences are not the result of brain dysfunction. Similar transformative effects are not seen after hallucinations from oxygen deprivation, narcotics, and acute psychotic events. These visions are just as real as math or language and just as useful in our everyday lives.

INTUITIONS WE ALL HAVE

Does this mean that to understand this point we have to wait until an angel in white or a dead relative appears? Absolutely not. Each person has only to examine his own life to recognize that we all have hunches, intuitions, and spiritual inspirations. They spring from the same source as the near-death experience. I challenged my most skeptical friend, asking him if it was true that he had never had a hunch or a feeling that came true. He readily acknowledged that he had, but did not think his hunch was comparable to the near-death experience.

One night he was stopped at a traffic light. The light turned green, but he experienced an overwhelming fear and nausea and could not go on. He felt he would have to pull over and be sick. As he started to do so, a car suddenly sped across the intersection against the red light. Had he driven at the green light, he might have been killed.

He had always assumed this was some sort of coincidence. Since he was not prone to nausea and had never had a feeling like this before, it was either a lucky one in a million coincidence or a precognitive sense of dread that saved his life.

As a researcher, I am confident this was not simply a coincidence. I have collected dozens of such stories. The warning of the impending accident can present itself in a number of different ways. Sometimes it is through a visual experience of an angel. Sometimes it is a voice saying "Don't go." Sometimes it is simply a feeling. Often, no reason is given. For my friend, it was through a visceral feeling of nausea. They can't all be coincidences.

The problem seems to be that what is a hunch or funny feeling to one person is a vision of a woman dressed in white to another. We need to become more aware of the possibility that we are all talking about the same thing, but arguing over the terms we use. I argue that if we see angels when we die, and those apparently are "real angels," why can't we see angels during other stages of life? Perhaps my friend's guardian angel had to kick him in the stomach to prevent him from crossing at the light. It is my opinion that the scientific evidence supports that statement more readily than his own opinion that he was saved by a coincidence of indigestion.

Pierre Jovanovic believes that an angel saved his life. He is a war correspondent for several well-known French magazines who has interviewed Idi Amin and covered the death of Ceausescu and the fall of Romania. I had a hard time understanding why he would spend his time investigating angel stories.

He told me that while driving alone through the wartorn streets of yet another hot spot in the world, he suddenly felt a hand push him down onto the passenger seat. At the same time, a sniper's bullet passed through his windshield and past his head. He would have been killed if he hadn't been pushed down on the seat.

He was shaken by the experience, not only to have come so close to death, but to have been saved by an unseen hand, without word or explanation. He began to speak with his fellow correspondents, and found that such stories were very common. He went on to write the definitive book on angels from the perspective of an investigative reporter. He told me that he concluded that angels are real, very powerful, and often very funny.

If it is true that people can interact with angels when they are dying, it follows naturally that we can interact with them during other phases of our life. The only other explanation for Pierre's story is that he was in fact saved by some sort of coincidence. We could suppose that he had some sort of seizure or involuntary muscle spasm that caused him to lurch sideways in his car, and that it was a matter of wonderful luck for him that it happened just as a sniper fired at him.

A skeptical materialistic worldview sees life as being a series of one in a million coincidences. After studying near-death experiences, I have become convinced that there are actually patterns to life that are manifested by events that seem to be coincidental.

I recognize that there is a danger in this line of thinking. It is too easy to assign meaning to events that are random. This is especially true in emotional situations in which we have a strong psychological need to believe in something, as can occur when we are faced with the death of people we love. I believe, however, that there is strong scientific support for my conclusion that there are physical and spiritual patterns that interconnect all of life.

Modern physicists teach us that life is light, of varying wavelengths. The building blocks of nature are not tiny atoms and molecules as I was taught in school. Instead, powerful electromagnetic forces unify everything we consider to be real. These forces bridge the enormous distances between the individual particles that make up matter, gaps relatively greater than the distances between the planets in our solar system. Even the earth itself has a powerful electromagnetic field that links it not only with all the biological organisms that live on it, but with the solar system and universe as well.

I have witnessed this electromagnetic link between the earth and human beings firsthand. Several years ago, we were drilling a new well for our home, as our old well had run dry. Nothing draws a crowd and conversation quicker than seeing a well driller's rig, at least in our neighborhood.

One of our neighbors stopped by to see what was happening. He told me that he was a dowser and could find water. If it is true that all of life is interconnected by underlying electromagnetic forces, then it is possible that some people can perceive the electromagnetic signature of water under the ground.

I asked him to point out where we could find water on our property. He became very embarrassed, and told me that he wasn't really a dowser, but that his father was, and that in order to find water, he would have to get his father's special wooden stick. I explained my theories to him, and confidently stated that if there was anything to dowsing at all, it came not from a stick but from our brain's ability to perceive the kind of "light" that came from hidden water.

I urged him to simply point to where the water was, relying on his intuition. He said, "Well, don't blame me if you hit a dry hole," and pointed. At the very spot he pointed to, the driller hit an artesian well that sent water spurting hundreds of feet into the air.

I believe that his ability to find water on my land was not a coincidence, but a dramatic illustration of the fact that all of life is physically interconnected through patterns of electro-magnetic energy. Scientists have recently found magnetic particles in our brains that may act as sensors of these unseen forces.

Many other examples of the unseen interconnections of the universe exist. Birds use the electromagnetic field of the earth and the energy fields of mountains to navigate. Human behavior is affected by sunspot activity. Carnival rides create thrills through centrifugal forces by tapping into the gravitational mass of distant stars.

I speculate that not only are there physical interconnections unifying the universe, but that there are spiritual interconnections as well. I believe that human consciousness and our perception of God are mediated by these same electromagnetic pathways. I recognize that this is a speculative leap on my part, and that not everyone will reach this same conclusion.

Nobel prize-winner Erwin Schrödinger reached a similar conclusion from his study of quantum physics. Albert Einstein expressed similar sentiments when he stated that "God does not play dice with the universe." Physician Deepak Chopra has extended this concept to what he calls "quantum healing," which represents a spiritual healing of the body at the sub-atomic level. Astrophysicist Stephen Hawking likewise comments that what he calls subatomic forces may well be the arena for the actions of God. Clearly, I am in good company when I make my intellectual leap.

The existence of unseen spiritual connections unifying life will be difficult to scientifically document. The one single message that I hear repeatedly from children who have died and lived to describe death is that they become convinced that a loving light from God unifies everything in life. That is, however, not scientific proof. Still, it is remarkable that this is a universal theme basic to those who have had near-death experiences, regardless of their prior religious background or spiritual beliefs. Their insights represent the only objective evidence of what it is like to die. This is why I have repeatedly emphasized that the scientific evidence concludes that their insights are the result of normal brain functioning, and are not the result of pathological hallucinations. I believe near-death experiences are real in the sense that we can believe and trust the information we gain from studying them.

NO COINCIDENCES

Ultimately, each person will have to make this decision for himself. I had the occasion to perform a mini-experiment on a seeming coincidence in my life. I had just returned from Holland, where I had been comparing research data with the famed Dutch cardiologist Wolfgang von Lommel. He is a near-death researcher and a firm believer that there are no coincidences in life. At the time, I politely disagreed with him, presenting the skeptical viewpoint that human beings simply assign meaning to random events.

When I returned home, I had occasion to browse through

my favorite old-book store, where I have often purchased old medical books, which I enjoy collecting. On this day, there was only one set of old books, a set of medical books in Dutch, which I could not read. I thought this was a funny coincidence, and then thought of my colleague's insistence that there were no coincidences.

So I purchased the books and sent them to him. My test was that if it was just a coincidence, then these books should have no meaning for Dr. von Lommel. But if he was correct, then these books would have some sort of special meaning for him, which in fact they did. He stated that these were a set of old medical texts that he had a particular interest in and had been looking for.

I now agree with Dr. von Lommel that when we dismiss these events as mere coincidence, we are dismissing and trivializing our own spiritual being. We cut ourselves off from a rich source of knowledge that we can use to understand our lives.

One of my patients was involved in a severe car accident that occurred when his mother was driving. He received extensive injuries and was scarred and crippled for life. Even though the mother was not at fault, she told me, "I have tried and convicted myself long ago."

She has been comforted, however, by a vivid vision she had several weeks before the accident. She had a lucid dream, unlike any she had ever had before. She suddenly awoke and realized that a presence was in her room. This presence was hard for her to describe, but seemed to be either an angel or perhaps her deceased mother. Although she could not give many details, she had a terrible knowledge that her son would be in an accident. At the end of the dream, she heard, in her mind, her son saying "Now I know how turtles feel." The experience was so real that she immediately went to check on her son. Later, when her son was in the hospital, a nurse came to the mother and said that he might have to be in a body cast, and the nurse said, "You know, he will look like a Ninja Turtle." The mother feels this presence was a guardian angel, and felt the presence again after the accident.

Her daughter told me that she thought that this "angel" came to warn of the impending accident. That is the typical sort of interpretation we might place on such a dream, and, in so doing, totally miss the point of it. Nothing in the dream was a warning. No details were given. There was no way the mother could have avoided the accident, short of never letting her son in a car again.

The real meaning of this dream is that this mother needed support at a terrible time in her life. The dream was not a warning or a prediction of the future, but rather a message that there is a purpose and pattern to life and that she and her family would survive their ordeal. This mother would not have traded this dream for a dozen precise dreams predicting stock market results, because of the insight and strength that she gained from it to accept her son's injuries. She understood the dream to mean that something terrible was going to happen, and that her family had a guardian angel who could provide emotional strength. The mother had a profound sense of peacefulness even immediately after the accident. She feels she could not have gone on without the understanding she received from this dream.

We trivialize and dismiss these visions because we cannot understand them. They are dismissed as coincidences unless they contain verifiable details that defy the natural laws of the universe. When we finally accept that this woman's dream was real, and that its purpose was not to help her to avoid her son's accident, but to be able to keep her family intact throughout the ordeal, we will start to understand the true nature of dreams and visions. Her son's accident has meaning. This knowledge has given his mother the will to survive.

My patient's mother told me that she accepted the reality of her dream after reading books on near-death experiences. I am convinced that her reasoning is sound. Once we accept that a light can come to us when we die, and that we can interact with that light, we must take the harder step of recognizing that that same light can interact with us at other times during our lives. In many ways, this is a harder concept to accept than life after death.

ONE CHANCE IN A THOUSAND

At a workshop for bereaved spouses, a woman told me about such a coincidence in her life. Several days after her husband's death, she received a postcard from her dentist reminding her of her routine checkup. When she examined the card, she gasped, as the picture on the postcard was of a special place in Washington for her and her husband. They traveled there when they first fell in love and thought of it as their special spot. She went to her appointment, and asked about the postcard. She was told that the dentist bought a series of postcards depicting hundreds of different scenes around Washington, and that it was just a one in a thousand chance that she received that card.

I told this story to my wife, and she immediately dismissed it as a coincidence. "Don't use that story in your book, that one really is a coincidence! I have a much better story than that."

She then proceeded to tell me something about her brother Chris's death that she had never shared with me before. After her brother died, she contacted all his old friends to tell them the news. One of them was a childhood friend named Romeo, who had not been in contact with the family in many years. He told her that her call was not unexpected. The night before her brother's death, Romeo had suddenly and inexplicably been thinking of Chris, and talked about him for hours. His girl-friend confirmed that he had been reminiscing about Chris all night, and that he had never really talked about him before.

Even my own wife does not believe that coincidences can sometimes illuminate a spiritual meaning in life. She is too busy raising five children to dwell on such things. Yet when I shared with her such a "meaningless coincidence," it immediately helped her to understand and recognize something important about her own brother's death. I would guess that most skeptics would also dismiss my wife's story as simply a coincidence, without meaning. If these same skeptics could keep an open mind, I am staking my scientific reputation that they will find similar coincidences that create meaning in their own lives.

After twelve years of cutting-edge research on near-death experiences, I still cannot say without a doubt that there is life after death. I do assert, without hesitation, that the widow's postcard from her dentist was not a coincidence. We cannot understand the importance of death-related visions in our lives unless we understand that there is something that is divine that exists independent of our own mind and body. This loving light, this God (for lack of a better word) can communicate with us and is communicating with us all the time. For those with natural right-temporal-lobe talents, the communication often comes in the form of an angel or being of light. For those people, like myself, who are right-temporal-lobe impaired, it is simply a hunch or an intuition or a kick in the gut. And yes, for some it will be a postcard from their dentist. It is through just this sort of divine coincidence that we can understand the meaning of our lives.

One of my medical school professors at Johns Hopkins University had a vision of a woman in white who explained to him that every life has a purpose and meaning. The child who dies at a young age from birth defects often knows a secret about life that those of us who live a little longer may never discover. Loving such children stretches our humanity, as does trusting that their lives, however short, are important.

Dr. Oski asked not that we believe his story, but rather make ourselves open to the many miracles happening around us. These miracles happen again and again on a daily basis. They are tiny miracles, miracles that do not impress talk show hosts or start religious crusades. The young widow's postcard from her dentist was one such miracle.

Don't wait for a vision of God or a glowing head to start to believe that your life has purpose and meaning. You have already experienced a miracle in your life.

AFTERWORD

—

And what if my experience was just a
farce, an ultimately meaningless experience? I
would rather have had my experience and died,
than to have lived without having it.

—Betty J. Eadie

Parting visions, the spiritual experiences surrounding death,
have the power to initiate a productive dialogue on the nature
of the human soul.

This is especially important in our society, in which so many
of our personal and social problems are basically afflictions of
the soul. Homelessness, racial hatred, gang warfare, a health
care system that wastes millions of dollars on heroic measures
for dying patients while depriving children of vaccinations—
these are all spiritual problems of our society that cannot be
fixed by laws or medications.

By confronting the fact of the existence of these parting visions we are reminded of our own spiritual nature. Even if
these experiences are not accepted as being proof of life after
death, they are without doubt a way of shedding light on our
own spirituality. They can even help us discover the meaning
of life, which is different for each of us.

Still most people are afraid of them.

A mayor of a small midwestern city told me a moving story that illustrates this point. Shortly after his daughter was killed in a boating accident, a young woman kept trying to contact him at his office. She told the members of his staff that she had a message for him from his dead daughter. Finally, after several attempts to reach him by telephone had failed, she showed up personally at his office and demanded to see him.

She told the mayor that she had been contacted by his dead daughter, who wanted him to know that she had left a message for him in her bedroom. He thanked the woman for this information and said he would look into it. Frankly, though, he had no intention of going into her room, which he had been unable to do since her death.

"I think she is just a nut," he told his staff when she left the office.

Several weeks later he ran into one of his daughter's friends on the street. The friend told the mayor about a dream he'd had only the week before. In the dream the mayor's daughter appeared at the foot of his bed and said to tell her dad that there was a message for him in her room.

The mayor could not ignore the second message. He immediately went to his daughter's room, where he found a poem that she had written only a few days before her death. The poem clearly indicated that she thought she was going to die soon and that everything would be all right.

Although the family is not particularly religious, the poem indicated that there was some kind of meaning to her death and that the family should not grieve for her.

This story is important because it documents the spiritual events that surround death. It is also important because it illustrates the fact that most of us don't want to face our spiritual nature.

Although this man was so intrigued by these death-related visions that he had to contact me, he feels that allowing me to use his name would hurt him politically. He emphasized that he has deliberately distanced himself from anything spiritual or religious in order to get votes and that he would alienate a great portion of the voting public if he were suddenly to acknowledge that a spiritual vision had touched him.

This attitude can be found among many people in our society. Doctors, nurses, scientists, policemen, ministers, and so on all recognize that even to discuss spirituality can diminish their own credibility.

Still, it is impossible to deny that we have a large area of our brain devoted to spiritual visions and psychical abilities. This area of our brain, the right temporal lobe and surrounding structures, is as large as our language center. The rich research on the brain indicates that this area can be activated in a number of different ways, from dying or experiencing the death of others to meditation. Sometimes it becomes activated for no apparent reason at all. It is this area of the brain that allows us to have visions, out-of-body experiences, and even the sorts of premonitions of death that more than 25 percent of the parents in the SIDS study had about their children.

Research into this whole field has proven that we have a portion of the brain that connects us with the divine. But are these experiences and the research surrounding them any proof of life after death? As far as I am concerned, the answer is yes. When I review the medical literature, I think it points directly to evidence that some aspect of human consciousness survives death. Other researchers agree with me. Physician Michael

Schroter-Kunhardt, for instance, conducted a comprehensive review of the scientific literature and concluded that "the paranormal capacities of the dying person suggest the existence of a time-and-space-transcending immortal soul." Other researchers have reached the same conclusions. Be it through case studies of their own or research they have reviewed, there is in the scientific community a growing belief in the human spirit.

But if you still have to make your own leap of faith, here is one final case study that might help you:

A man in Washington State was killed when his car skidded off the road and hit a tree. His brother-in-law was fishing at the time of the accident in a remote area and was unaware of the accident.

Late in the afternoon the man who was fishing suddenly encountered his dead brother-in-law walking down the path toward his fishing hole. The man was glad to have company. They spoke for several minutes until the visitor said that he had to leave and walked quickly into the woods and disappeared.

The man who was fishing said the experience was so vivid that it took him several minutes to realize that his brother-in-law could not have been there. He returned home, where his sister told him of her husband's death.

This case study doesn't end there. The man still "visits" his family often. He was a carpenter by trade and visits his wife's son frequently with helpful suggestions about woodworking projects.

The family is not alarmed by these visits. Like so many others, they find these visions a source of help and comfort.

BIBLIOGRAPHY

Adair, D. K., and Keshavan, M. S. "The Charles Bonnet Syndrome and Grief Reaction" (letter). *American Journal of Psychiatry* 145 (1988): 895–96.

Ader, R.; Felten, D. L.; Cohen, N. (eds). *Psychoneuroimmunology.* New York: Academic Press, 1991: 3–25, 847–932.

Alroe, C. J., and McIntyre, J. N. M. "Visual Hallucinations: The Charles Bonnet Syndrome and Bereavement." *Medical Journal of Australia* 2 (1983): 674–75.

Alvarado, C. "The Psychological Approach to Out-of-Body Experiences: A Review of Early and Modern Developments." *Journal of Psychology* 126 (1992): 237–50.

Anonymous. "It's Over Debbie." *JAMA* 259 (1988): 272.

Appleby, L. "Near-Death Experience: Analogous to Other Stress-Induced Psychological Phenomena." *British Medical Journal* 298 (1989): 976–77.

Aries, P. *The Hour of Our Death.* New York: Alfred A. Knopf, 1981: 559–616.

Audette, J. R. "Historical Perspectives on Near-Death Experiences and Episodes." In Lundahl, C. R. (ed), *A Collection of Near-Death Readings.* Chicago: Nelson Hall Publishers, 1982: 21–46.

Balk, D. "Adolescents, Grief Reactions and Self-Concept Perceptions Following Sibling Death: A Study of 33 Teenagers." *Journal of Youth and Adolescence* 12 (1983): 137–59.

Barrett, E. A. M.; Doyle, M. B.; Malinski, V. M.; et al. "The Relationship Among the Experience of Dying, the Experience of Paranormal Events, and Creativity in Adults." In Barrett, E. A. M. (ed), *Visions of Rogers' Science-Based Nursing*. National League for Nursing Publication No. 15-2285, New York, 1990.

Barrett, Sir William. *Deathbed Visions: The Psychical Experiences of Dying*. The Aquarian Press, 1986 (reprint of 1926 edition).

Bates, B. C., and Stanley, A. "The Epidemiology and Differential Diagnosis of Near-Death Experience." *American Journal of Orthopsychiatry* 55 (1985): 542–49.

Becker, C. B. "The Pure Land Revisited: Sin-Japanese Meditations and Near-Death Experiences of the Next World." *Anabiosis: The Journal of Near-Death Studies* 4 (1984): 51–68.

Becker, E. *The Denial of Death*. New York: Free Press, 1973.

Bender, L., and Lipkowitz, H. H. "Hallucinations in Children." *American Journal of Orthopsychiatry* 10 (1940): 334–43.

Blacher, R. S. "The Hidden Psychosis of Open-Heart Surgery: With a Note on the Sense of Awe." *JAMA* 222 (1972): 305–8.

Blackmore, S. "Out-of-Body Experiences in Schizophrenia." *Journal of Nervous and Mental Disorders* 174 (1986): 615–19.

———."Visions from the Dying Brain." *New Scientist* 5 (May 1988): 43–46.

Bluebond-Langer, M. "Meanings of Death to Children." In Felfel, H. (ed), *New Meanings of Death*. New York: McGraw-Hill, 1977: 47–66.

———. *The Private Worlds of Dying Children*. Princeton, New Jersey: Princeton University Press, 1978: 198–235.

Bonnet, C. *Essai Analytique sur les Facultés de l'Ame*, vol. 2, 2nd ed. Copenhagen and Geneva: Philbert, 1976: 176–77.

Bret, P. T. *Les métapsychoses: la métapsychorragie, la télépathic, la hantise. Vol I: Introduction and Phantasmal Métapsychorrhagy*. Paris: J. B. Bailliere, 1939.

Broughton, R. *Parapsychology: The Controversial Science*. New York: Ballantine, 1991.

Brown, D. R.; Meyer, P. C.; Shifrin, D. L.; et al. "Pediatrics and

Death: A Compassion Deficit?" *Pediatric Management* (July 1993): 13–29.

Budge, E. A. W. *The Egyptian Book of the Dead.* New York: Dover Publications, 1967: lx–lxviii.

Burch, G. E.; DePasquale, N. P.; Phillips, J. H. "What Death Is Like." *American Heart Journal* 76 (1968): 438–39.

Butt, W.; Shann, F.; Tibballs, J.; et al. "Long-Term Outcome of Children After Intensive Care." *Critical Care Medicine* 18 (1990): 961–64.

Calvin, W. *The Cerebral Symphony: Seashore Reflections on the Structure of Consciousness.* New York: Bantam Books, 1990: 51–54.

Campbell, J. *Creative Mythology: The Masks of God.* Harrisonburg, Virginia: Penguin Books, 1968.

———. *Myths to Live By.* New York: Bantam Books, 1972.

———. *The Power of Myth.* New York: Doubleday, 1984: 163–71.

———. *Primitive Mythology.* Harrisonburg, Va.: Penguin Books, 1967.

Carr, C. "Death and Near-Death: A Comparison of Tibetan and Euro-American Experiences." *Journal of Transpersonal Psychology* 25 (1993): 59–110.

Carr, D. "Pathophysiology of Stress-Induced Limbic Lobe Dysfunction: A Hypothesis for NDEs." *Anabiosis: The Journal of Near-Death Studies* 2 (1982): 75–90.

Cavendish, R. *Visions of Heaven and Hell.* New York: Harmony Books, 1977: 1–45.

Chesler, M. A.; Paris, J.; Barbarin, O. A. " 'Telling' the Child with Cancer: Parental Choices to Share Information with Ill Children." *Pediatric Psychology* 11 (1986): 497–516.

Comer, N. L.; Madow, L.; Dixon, J. J. "Observations of Sensory Deprivation in a Life-Threatening Situation." *American Journal of Psychiatry* 124 (1967): 164–70.

Corcoran, D. K. "Helping Patients Who've Been Near Death." *Nursing '88* 11 (1988): 34–39.

Crawford, S. W., and Petersen, B. F. "Long-Term Survival from Respiratory Failure After Marrow Transplantation for Malignancy." *American Review of Respiratory Diseases* 145 (1992): 510–14.

Crookiall, R. *The Supreme Adventure.* London: James Clarke, 1961.

de Vesme, C. Review of "The Case for Astral Projection" by Muldoon, S. J. *Revue métapsychique* 23 (1934): 224–25.

Dobson, M.; Tallersfield, A. E.; Adler, M. W.; et al. "Attitudes and Long-Term Adjustment of Patients Surviving Cardiac Arrest." *British Medical Journal* 3 (1971): 207–12.

Doore, G. *What Survives Contemporary Explorations of Life After Death.* Los Angeles: Jeremy Tarcher, 1990.

Dossey, L. *Meaning and Medicine.* New York: Bantam, 1991: 99–273.

Dougherty, C. M. "The Near-Death Experience as a Major Life Transition." *Holistic Nursing Practice* 4 (1990): 84–90.

Druss, R. G., and Kornfield, D. S. "The Survivors of Cardiac Arrest: A Psychiatric Study." *JAMA* 201 (1967): 291–96.

Egbert, L. D. "Reduction of Postoperative Pain by Encouragement and Instruction of Patients." *New England Journal of Medicine* 278 (1964): 825–27.

Ehrenwald, J. "Out-of-Body Experiences and the Denial of Death." *Journal of Nervous and Mental Disorders* 159 (1974): 227–33.

Eliade, M. *Shamanism: Archaic Techniques of Ecstasy.* Princeton, N.J.: Princeton University Press, 1992.

Florell, J. L. "Crisis Intervention in Orthopedic Surgery—Empirical Evidence of the Effectiveness of a Chaplain Working with Surgery Patients." *Bulletin of the American Hospital Association* 37 (1973): 29–36.

Frazer, J. *The New Golden Bough.* New York: New American Library, 1959.

Gabbard, G. O., and Twemlow, S. W. *With the Eyes of the Mind: An Empirical Analysis of Out-of-Body States.* New York: Praeger, 1984: 3–45, 154–69.

Gardner, G. G. "Childhood, Death and Human Dignity: Hypnotherapy for David." *International Journal of Clinical Hypnotherapy* 24 (1976): 122–39.

Gardner, J., and Maier, J. *Gilgamesh*. New York: Vintage Books, 1985.

Gardner, R. "Miracles of Healing in Anglo-Celtic Northumbria as Recorded by the Venerable Bede and his Contemporaries: A Reappraisal in the Light of Twentieth-Century Experience." *British Medical Journal* 287 (1983): 24–31.

Garralda, M. E. "Hallucinations in Psychiatrically Disordered Children: Preliminary Communication." *J Roy Soc Med* 75 (1982): 181–84.

Gaumer, G. L., and Stavins, J. "Medicare Use in the Last 90 Days of Life." *Health Serv Res* 26 (1992): 725–42.

Glass, N. L.; Murray, P. A.; Ruttimann, U. E. "Pediatric Intensive Care: Who, Why and How Much." *Critical Care Medicine* 14 (1986): 222–26.

Greaves, G. B. "Multiple Personality 165 Years After Mary Reynolds." *Journal of Nervous and Mental Disorders* 168 (1980): 577–96.

Grey, M. *Return from Death: An Exploration of the Near-Death Experience*. London: Arkana, 1985: 147–69.

Greyson, B. "The Near-Death Experience Scale: Construction, Reliability and Validity." *Journal of Nervous and Mental Disorders* 171 (1983): 360–75.

———. "Near-Death Experiences and Personal Values." *American Journal of Psychiatry* 140 (1983): 618–20.

Greyson, B., and Bush, N. E. "Distressing Near-Death Experiences." *Psychiatry* 55 (1992): 95–110.

Greyson, B., and Stevenson, I. "Near-Death Experiences." *JAMA* 242 (1979): 265–67.

———. "The Phenomenology of Near-Death Experiences." *American Journal of Psychiatry* 137 (1980): 1193–95.

Grimby, A. "Bereavement Among Elderly People: Grief Reactions,

Post-Bereavement Hallucinations and Quality of Life." *Acta Psychiatr Scand* 87 (1993): 72–80.

Grof, S., and Halifax, J. "The Human Encounter with Death." In *Psychedelic biographies*. New York: E. P. Dutton, 1963: 63–108.

Gruen, A. "Relationship of Sudden Infant Death and Parental Unconscious Conflicts." *Pre- and Perinatal Psychology Journal* 2 (1987): 50–56.

Hackett, T. P. "The Lazarus Complex Revisited." *Annals of Internal Medicine* 76 (1972): 135–37.

Hagemaster, J. N. "Life History: A Qualitative Method of Research." *Journal of Advanced Nursing* 17 (1992): 1122–28.

Halgren, E.; Walter, R. D.; Cherlow, D. G.; et al. "Mental Phenomena Evoked by Electrical Stimulation of the Human Hippocampal Formation and Amygdala." *Brain* 101 (1978): 83–117.

Hallowell, I. "Spirits of the Dead in Saulteaux Life and Thought." *J Roy Anthropol Inst* 70 (1940): 29–51.

Haraldsson, E. "Survey of Claimed Encounters with the Dead." *Omega* 19 (1988–89): 103–13.

Harner, M. *The Way of the Shaman*. New York: Harper, 1990: 1–56, 95–113.

Heim, A. "Notizen uber den tod durch absturz." *Jahrbuch des Schweizer Alpenclubs* 27 (1892): 327–37. Translated by Noyes, R., and Kletti, R. "The Experience of Dying from Falls." *Omega* (1972): 45–52.

Hennsley, J. A.; Christenson, P. J.; Hairdoin, R. A.; et al. "Premonitions of Sudden Infant Death Syndrome: A Retrospective Case Control Study." Presented at the National SIDS Alliance Meeting, Pittsburgh, October 1993 (abstract). *Pediatric Pulmonology* 16 (1993): 393.

Hertzog, D. B., and Herrin, J. T. "Near-Death Experiences in the Very Young." *Critical Care Medicine* 13 (1985): 1074–75.

Hooper, J., and Teresi, D. *The 3-Pound Universe: The Brain*. New York: Dell Publishing, 1986: 324–36.

Horrax, G. "Visual Hallucinations as a Cerebral Localizing Phenomenon: With Special Reference to Their Occurrence in Tumors of the Temporal Lobes." *Archives of Neurological Psychiatry* 10 (November 1923): 532–47.

Houlberg, L. "Coming Out of the Dark." *Nursing '92* (February 1992): 43.

Hufford, D. J. "Paranormal Experiences in the General Population: A Commentary." *Journal of Nervous and Mental Disorders* 180 (1992): 362–68.

Hunter, R. C. A. "On the Experience of Nearly Dying." *American Journal of Psychiatry* 124 (1967): 122–23.

Irwin, H. J. "The Psychological Function of Out-of-Body Experiences." *Journal of Nervous and Mental Disorders* 169 (1981): 244–48.

Iverson, J. *In Search of the Dead: A Scientific Investigation of Evidence of Life After Death.* San Francisco: Harper, 1992: 3–203.

Jansen, K. R. "The Near-Death Experience" (letter). *Lancet* 153 (1988): 883–84.

Johnsen, A. R. "To Help the Dying Die—A New Duty for Anesthesiologists?" *Anesthesiology* 78 (1993): 225–28.

Judson, J. R., and Wiltshaw, E. "A Near-Death Experience." *Lancet* 2 (1983): 561–62.

Jung, C. *Memories, Dreams and Reflections.* New York: Random House, 1961.

Kalish, R. A. "An Approach to Death Attitudes." *American Behavioral Sciences* 6 (1963): 68.

———. "The Effects of Death upon the Family." In Pearson, L. (ed). *Death and Dying: Current Issues in the Treatment of the Dying Patient.* Cleveland: Case Western Reserve University Press, 1969: 79–101.

Kalish, R. A., and Reynolds, D. K. "Phenomenological Reality and Post-Death Contact." *Journal for the Scientific Study of Religion* (1973): 209–21.

Kastenbaum, R. "Transformed by the Light" (book review). *Journal of Near-Death Studies* 12 (1993).

Katz, N. M.; Agle, D. P.; DePalma, R. G.; et al. "Delirium in Surgical Patients Under Intensive Care." *Archives of Surgery* 104 (1972): 310–13.

Kellehear, A. "Culture, Biology and the Near-Death Experience: A Reappraisal." *Journal of Nervous and Mental Disorders* 181 (1993): 148–56.

———. "The Near-Death Experience as Status Passage." *Soc Sci Med* 31 (1990): 933–39.

Knaus, W. A.; Wagner, D. P.; Lynn, J. "Short-Term Mortality Predictions for Critically Ill Hospitalized Adults: Science and Ethics." *Science* 254 (1991): 389–94.

Kohr, R. L. "Near-Death Experiences, Altered States and Psi Sensitivity." *Anabiosis: The Journal of Near-Death Studies* 3 (1983): 157–76.

Komp, D. M. *A Window to Heaven: When Children See Life in Death.* Grand Rapids, Michigan: Zondervan Publishing, 1992.

Kroll, J., and Bachrach, B. "Visions and Psychopathology in the Middle Ages." *Journal of Nervous and Mental Disorders* 170 (1982): 41–49.

Kübler-Ross, E. *On Children and Death.* New York: Macmillan Publishing, 1983.

Kutscher, A. H. (ed). *Death and Bereavement.* Springfield, Ill.: Charles C. Thomas, 1969: 84–98.

Lanios, J. D.; Miles, S. H.; Silverstein, M. D.; et al. "Survival After Cardiopulmonary Resuscitation in Babies of Very Low Birth Weight: Is CPR Futile Therapy?" *New England Journal of Medicine* (1988): 318–91.

Lee, A. "The Lazarus Syndrome: Caring for Patients Who Have Returned from the Dead." *RN* 41 (1978): 53–64.

Markson, Leona, replies: Her 7-year-old son with AMI, status post-bone marrow transplant, now discharged [letter]. *JAMA* 269 (1993): 2738–39.

Leming, M. R., and Dickinson, G. E. *Understanding Dying, Death, and Bereavement.* Orlando, Fla.: Holt, Rinehart & Winston, 1990: 93–139.

Levin, C., and Curley, M. *Near-Death Experiences in Children.* Reported at "Perspective on Change: Forces Shaping Practice for the Clinical Nurse Specialist," Boston Children's Hospital, October 11, 1990.

Lewis, D. "All in Good Faith." *Nursing Times* 83 (1987): 40–43.

Lisansky, J.; Strassman, R. J.; Janowsky, D.; et al. "Drug-Induced Psychoses." In Tupin, J. P.; Halbreich, U.; Pena, J. J. (eds), *Transient Psychosis: Diagnosis, Management and Evaluation.* New York: Bruner/Mazel, 1984: 80–111.

Littlewood, J. *Aspects of Grief: Bereavement in Adult Life.* Nashville, Tenn.: Tavistock Tyson Rutledge Press, 1992: 112–37.

Locke, T. P., and Shontz, F. C. "Personality Correlates of the Near-Death Experience: A Preliminary Study." *Journal of the American Society for Psychical Research* 77 (1983): 311–18.

Loftus, E. *Witness for the Defense.* New York: St. Martin's Press, 1991: 14–30, 250–51.

Lundahl, C. R. "Near-Death Experiences of Mormons." In Lundahl, C. R. (ed). *A Collection of Near-Death Readings.* Chicago: Nelson Hall Publishers, 1982: 165–79.

McCuster, J. "Where Cancer Patients Die: An Epidemiologic Study." *Public Health Report* 98 (1983): 170–76.

MacMillan, R. L., and Brown, K. W. G. "Cardiac Arrest Remembered." *Canadian Medical Association Journal* 104 (1971): 889–90.

McSherry, E.; Kratz, D.; Nelson, W. A. "Pastoral Care Departments: More Necessary in the DRG Era." *Health Care Management Review* 11 (1986): 47–61.

Maitz, E. A., and Pekala, R. J. "Phenomenological Quantification of an Out-of-Body Experience Associated with a Near-Death Event." *Omega* 22 (1990–91): 199–214.

Mandell, A. "Toward a Psychobiology of Transcendence: God in the Brain." In Davidson, Davidson (eds). *The Psychobiology of Consciousness.* New York: Plenum Press, 1980: 54–86.

Mant, A. K. "The Medical Definition of Death." In Shneidman, E.

(ed). *Death: Current Perspectives.* Palo Alto, Ca.: Mayfield Publishing, 1976: 144–86.

Matchett, W. F. "Repeated Hallucinatory Experiences as a Part of the Mourning Process Among Hopi Indian Women." *Psychiatry* 35 (1972): 185–94.

Mendelsohn, D.; McDonald, D. W.; Nogueira, C.; et al. "Anesthesia for Open-Heart Surgery." *Anesth Analg* 39 (1960): 110–20.

Merkawah. *Research: Progress Report on the Research into Near-Death Experiences.* Loosdrecht, Netherlands, [International Association for Near-Death Studies, Netherlands]. January 1990.

Miles, M. B., and Huberman, A. M. *Qualitative Data Analysis: A Sourcebook of New Methods.* Newbury Park, Ca.: Sage Publications, 1984: 15–27.

Miles, M. S., and Demi, A. S. "Toward the Development of a Theory of Bereavement Guilt: Sources of Guilt in Bereaved Parents." *Omega* 14 (1983–84): 299–314.

Mogenson, G. *Greeting the Angels: An Imaginal View of the Mourning Process.* Amityville, N.Y.: Baywood Publishing, 1992.

Moody, R. *Life After Death.* New York: Bantam Books, 1975: 1–26.

———. "Near-Death Experiences: Dilemma for the Clinician." *Virginia Med* 104 (1977): 687–90.

Morse, M. L. "Death Related Visions of Childhood: Theoretical Implications for the Clinician." *Journal of Pediatric Oncology Nursing* (in press).

———. "A Near-Death Experience in a 7-Year-Old Child." *American Journal of Diseases in Children* 137 (1983): 959–61.

Morse, M. L., and Neppe, V. M. "Near-Death Experiences" [letter]. *Lancet* 337 (1991): 386.

Morse, M. L., and Perry, P. *Closer to the Light.* New York: Villard Books, 1990: 110.

———. *Transformed by the Light.* New York: Villard, 1992: 29–61, 170–74, 212–13.

Morse, M. L.; Castillo, P.; Venecia, D. "Childhood Near-Death Experiences." *American Journal of Diseases in Children* 140 (1986): 110–14.

Morse, M. L.; Venecia, D.; Milstein, J. M. "Near-Death Experiences: A Neurophysiological Explanatory Model." *Anabiosis: The Journal of Near-Death Studies* 8 (1989): 45–54.

Murphy, P. A., and Albers, L. L. "Evaluation of Research Studies: Part II: Observational Studies." *Journal of Nurse Midwifery* 37 (1992): 411–13.

Nagy, M. "The Child's View of Death." *J Genet Psychology* 7 (1948): 3–27.

Negovsky, V. A. "Reanimatology Today." *Critical Care Medicine* 10 (1982): 130–33.

———. *Resuscitation and Artificial Hypothermia*. New York Consultants Bureau, 1962.

Neppe, V. M. "Temporal Lobe Symptomatology in Subjective Paranormal Experiences." *Journal of the American Society for Psychical Research* 77 (1983): 1–29.

Nitschke, R.; Humphrey, G. B.; Sexauer, C. L.; et al. "Therapeutic Choices Made by Patients with End-Stage Cancer." *Journal of Pediatrics* 101 (1982): 471–74.

Noyes, R. "Attitude Change Following Near-Death Experiences." *Psychiatry* 43 (1980): 234–42.

———. "Near-Death Experiences: Their Interpretation and Significance." In Kastenbaum, R., *Between Life and Death*. New York: Springer Publishing, 1979: 73–88.

Noyes, R., and Kletti, R. "Depersonalization in the Face of Life-Threatening Danger: A Description." *Psychiatry* 39 (1976): 19–27.

Noyes, R.; Hoenk, P. R.; Kuperman, S.; et al. "Depersonalization in Accident Victims and Psychiatric Patients." *Journal of Nervous and Mental Disorders* 164 (1977): 401–7.

Oakes, A. "The Lazarus Syndrome: A Care Plan for the Unique Needs of Those Who've Died." *RN* 41 (1978): 60–64.

Olson, M. "Near-Death Experiences and the Elderly." *Holistic Nurse Practitioner* 7 (1992): 16–21.

———. "The Out-of-Body Experience and Other States of Consciousness." *Archives of Psychiatric Nursing* 1 (1987): 201–7.

Omer, H. ["Dar Reuven."] Changing Trends in Three Decades of Psychotherapy Research: The Flight from Theory into Pragmatics." *J Consult Clin Psychol* 60 (1992): 88–93.

Osis, K., and Harroldsson, E. *At the Hour of Death.* New York: Avon Books, 1977.

Oski, F. A. "An Epiphany?" *Contemporary Pediatrics* 10 (1993): 9–10.

Owens, J. E.; Cook, E. W.; Stevenson, I. "Features of Near-Death Experience in Relation to Whether or Not Patients Were Near Death." *Lancet* 336 (1990): 1175–77.

Oye, R. K., and Bellamy, P. E. "Patterns of Resource Consumption in Medical Intensive Care." *Chest* 99 (1991): 685–89.

Papadatou, D., and Papadatou, C. *Children and Death.* New York: Hemisphere Publishing Corp., 1991.

Penfield, W. "Functional Localization in Temporal and Deep Sylvian Areas." In Solomon, H. C.; Cobb, S.; Penfield, W. (eds) (research publications). *New York Association for Research in Nervous and Mental Disease* 36 (1954): 210–26.

———. "The Role of Temporal Cortex in Certain Psychical Phenomena." *J Ment Sci* 101 (1955): 451–65.

Penfield, W., and Rasmussen, T. *The Cerebral Cortex of Man: A Clinical Study of Localization of Function.* New York: Macmillan, 1950: 162–81.

Persinger, M. "Religious and Mystical Experiences as Artifacts of Temporal Lobe Function: A General Hypothesis." *Percept Motor Skills* 57 (1983): 1255–62.

Pfister, O. "Schockdenken und Schock phantasien bei höchster Todesgefahr." *Zschr Psa* 16 (1930): 430–55.

Pierce, C. S. *A Crack in the Cosmic Egg.* New York: Pocket Books, 1971: 177.

Plum, F. P., and Posner, J. B. *Diagnosis of Stupor and Coma,* 2nd ed. Contemporary Neurology Series. Philadelphia: F. A. Davis Co., 1972: 2–25, 236–39.

Pollack, M. M.; Wilkinson, J. D.; Glass, N. L. "Long Stay Pediatric

Intensive Care Unit Patients: Outcome and Resource Utilization." *Pediatrics* 80 (1987): 855–60.

Rando, T. *Parental Loss of a Child.* Champaign, Ill.: Research Press, 1986: 3–118, 166.

Rawlings, M. *Before Death Comes.* Nashville, Tenn.: Nelson, 1980.

———. *Beyond Death's Door.* Nashville, Tenn.: Nelson, 1978.

Rees, W. D. "The Hallucinations of Widowhood." *British Medical Journal* 4 (1971): 37–41.

Ring, K. *Heading Toward Omega: In Search of the Meaning of the Near-Death Experience.* New York: William Morrow, 1984: 252–69.

———. *Life at Death: A Scientific Investigation.* New York: Quill, 1982: 27–39, 265–70.

———. *Near-Death Experiences: UFOs and Mind-at-Large.* New York: Macmillan, 1992.

Ring, K., and Lawrence, M. "Further Evidence for Veridical Perception During Near-Death Experiences." *Anabiosis: The Journal of Near-Death Studies* 11(4) (1993): 223–29.

Roberts, G., and Owen, J. "The Near-Death Experience." *British Journal of Psychiatry* 153 (1988): 607–17.

Rothenberg, J. *Technicians of the Sacred.* New York: Anchor Books, 1969: 92–98.

Rothenberg, M. "The Dying Child." In Call, J. D.; Noshpitz, J. D.; Cohen, R. L.; et al. (eds), *Basic Handbook of Child Psychiatry.* New York: Basic Books, 1979.

Sabom, M. B. *Recollections of Death: A Medical Investigation.* New York: Harper & Row, 1982: 1–14, 80–115.

Sabom, M. B., and Kreutiger, S. A. "Physicians Evaluate the Near-Death Experience." *Journal of the Florida Medical Association* 6 (1978): 1–6.

Sagan, C. *Broca's Brain.* New York: Random House, 1979: 65–88.

Schapira, D. V.; Studnicki, J.; Bradham, D. D. "Intensive Care, Survival and Expense of Treating Critically Ill Cancer Patients." *JAMA* 269 (1993): 783–86.

Schenk, L., and Bear, D. "Multiple Personality and Related Dissociative Phenomena in Patients with Temporal Lobe Epilepsy." *American Journal of Psychiatry* 138 (1981): 1311–16.

Schnaper, N. "The Psychological Implications of Severe Trauma: Emotional Sequelae to Unconsciousness." *Journal of Trauma* 15 (1975): 94–98.

Schoenbeck, S. B. "Exploring the Mystery of Near-Death Experiences." *American Journal of Nursing* 93 (1993): 43–46.

Schoonmaker, F. "Near-Death Experiences." *Anabiosis: The Journal of Near-Death Studies* 1 (1979): 1–35.

Schroter-Kunhardt, M. "Erfahrungen sterbender während des klinischen Todes." *Zeitschrift Fur Allgemeinmedizin* 66 (1990): 1014–21.

———. "A Review of Near-Death Experiences." *J Soc Sci Exp* 7 (1993): 219–39.

Schuster, D. P. "Everything that Should Be Done—Not Everything that Can Be Done." *American Review of Respiratory Diseases* 145 (1992): 508–10.

Sekaer, C. "Toward a Definition of Childhood Mourning." *American Journal of Psychotherapy* 41 (1987): 200–19.

Serdahely, W. "Pediatric Death Experiences." *Anabiosis: The Journal of Near-Death Studies* 9 (1990): 33–41.

Serdahely, W.; Drenk, A.; Serdahely, J. J. "What Carers Need to Understand About the Near-Death Experience." *Geriatric Nursing* 9 (1988): 238–41.

Shackleton, C. H. "The Psychology of Grief: A Review." *Adv Behav Ther* 6 (1984): 153–205.

Sidgewick, H. "Report on the Consensus of Hallucinations." *Proceedings of the Society for Psychical Research* 10 (1894): 25–422.

Siegel, K., and Weinstein, L. "Anticipatory Grief Reconsidered." *Journal of Psychosocial Oncology* 1 (1983): 61–73.

Siegel, R. K. "The Psychology of Life After Death." *Am Psychol* 35 (1980): 911–31.

Simonds, J. F. "Hallucinations in Non-Psychotic Children." *British Journal of Psychiatry* 129 (1975): 267–76.

Spiegel, D.; Bloom, J.; Kraemer, H.; et al. "Effects of Psychosocial Treatment on Survivors of Patients with Metastatic Breast Cancer." *Lancet* 2 (1989): 888–91.

Spiegel, R. K., and Jarvik, M. E. "Drug-Induced Hallucinations in Animals and Man." In Siegel, R. K.; West, L. J. (eds), *Hallucinations: Behavior, Experience and Theory*. New York: John Wiley & Sons, 1975: 178–212.

Spitzner, M. *Halluzinationen: Ein Beitrag zur allgemeinen und klinischen Psychopathologic*. Berlin, Heidelberg: Springer Verlag, 1988.

Stack-O'Sullivan, D. J. "Personality Correlates of Near-Death Experiences." 1981 Dissertation, *Abstracts International* 42 (1981): 2584-A.

Staudacher, C. *Beyond Grief*. Oakland, Ca.: New Harbinger Publications, 1987: 132–33.

Stevenson, I. "Do We Need a New Word to Supplement 'Hallucination'?" *American Journal of Psychiatry* 140 (1983): 1609–11.

Swedenborg, E. *Heaven and Hell*. New York: Swedenborg Foundation, 1928.

Taylor, G. R. *The Natural History of the Mind*. London: Penguin Books, 1979.

Thompson, K. *Angels and Aliens: UFOs and the Mythic Imagination*. New York: Fawcett Columbine, 1991: 48–62.

Tobacyk, J. "Death Threat, Death Concerns, and Paranormal Belief." *Death Education* 7 (1983): 115–24.

Torphy, D. E.; Minter, M. G.; Thompson, B. M. "Cardiorespiratory Arrest and Resuscitation of Children." *American Journal of Diseases in Children* 138 (1984): 1099–1102.

Tosch, P. "Patients' Recollections of their Posttraumatic Coma." *Journal of Neuroscientific Nursing* 20 (1988): 223–28.

Trevelyan, J. "Near-Death Experiences." *Nursing Times* 85 (1989): 39–41.

Truog, R. D., and Berde, C. B. "Pain, Euthanasia, and Anesthesiologists." *Anesthesiology* 78 (1993): 353–60.

Vachon, M. L. S. *Occupational Stress in the Care of the Critically Ill, the Dying and the Bereaved.* Bristol, Pa.: Hemisphere Publishing Corp., 1987: 1–39.

Van Buren, J. M. "Sensory, Motor and Automatic Effects of Mesial Temporal Stimulation in Man." *Journal of Neurosurgery* 18 (1961): 273–88.

VanCott, M. L.; Tittle, M. B.; Moody, L. F.; et al. "Analysis of a Decade of Critical Care Nursing Practice Research: 1979–1988." *Heart Lung* 21 (1991): 394–97.

Vicchio, S. "Near-Death Experiences: A Critical Review of the Literature and some Questions for Further Study." *Essence* 5 (1981): 79.

Walker, F. O. "A Nowhere-Near-Death Experience: Heavenly Choirs Interrupt Myelography" [letter]. *JAMA* 261 (1989): 1282–89.

Warmington, E. R., and Rouse, P. G. (eds). *Great Dialogues of Plato: The Republic, Book X,* translated by W. N. D. Rouse. New York: New American Library, 1984.

West, L. J. "A Clinical and Theoretical Overview of Hallucinatory Phenomena." In Siegel, R. K., and West, L. J. (eds), *Hallucinations: Behavior, Experience and Theory.* New York: John Wiley & Sons, 1975: 77–112.

Will, G. *Men at Work: The Craft of Baseball.* New York: Macmillan, 1990.

Worden, W. J. *Grief Counseling and Grief Therapy,* 2nd ed. New York: Springer Publishing, 1991.

Yates, T. T., and Bannard, J. R. "The Haunted Child: Grief, Hallucinations and Family Dynamics." *Journal of the American Academy of Child and Adolescence* 27 (1988): 573–81.

Zaleski, C. *Otherworld Journeys.* New York: Oxford University Press, 1987: 26–45, 107.

ABOUT THE AUTHORS

MELVIN MORSE, M.D., and PAUL PERRY have written the bestsellers *Closer to the Light* and *Transformed by the Light*. Morse is a practicing pediatrician in Seattle, Washington. Perry is the former executive editor of *American Health* magazine and lives in Scottsdale, Arizona.